Language
Arts

Grade 4

Flash Kids

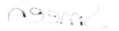

Harcourt Family Learning™

© 2005 by Flash Kids
Adapted from *Language Arts, Grade 4*
© 2003 by Harcourt Achieve
Licensed under special arrangement with Harcourt Achieve.

Illustrated by Remy Simard

ISBN: 978-1-4114-0412-0

Please submit all inquiries to FlashKids@bn.com

Printed and bound in Canada

Lot #:
18 20 22 23 21 19
10/13

Flash Kids
A Division of Barnes & Noble
122 Fifth Avenue
New York, NY 10011

Dear Parent,

This book was developed to help your child improve the language skills he or she needs to succeed. The book emphasizes skills in the key areas of:

- grammar
- punctuation
- vocabulary
- writing
- research

The more than 100 lessons included in the book provide many opportunities for your child to practice and apply important language and writing skills. These skills will help your child improve his or her communication abilities, excel in all academic areas, and increase his or her scores on standardized tests.

About the Book

The book is divided into six units:

- Parts of Speech
- Sentences
- Mechanics
- Vocabulary and Usage
- Writing
- Research Skills

Your child can work through each unit of the book, or you can pinpoint areas for extra practice.

Lessons have specific instructions and examples and are designed for your child to complete independently. Grammar lessons range from using nouns and verbs to constructing better sentences. Writing exercises range from the friendly letter to the research report. With this practice, your child will gain extra confidence as he or she works on daily school lessons or standardized tests.

A thorough answer key is also provided so you may check the quality of answers.

A Step toward Success

Practice may not always make perfect, but it is certainly a step in the right direction. The activities in this book are an excellent way to ensure greater success for your child.

Table of Contents

Unit 3: Mechanics

Unit 4: Vocabulary and Usage

Unit 5: Writing

Unit 6: Research Skills

Nouns

> A **noun** is a word that names a person, place, or thing.
> Use exact nouns to make clear pictures.
> *Examples:*
> person = woman   place = library   thing = chair

DIRECTIONS ⟶ Underline each noun. Then, replace the word in dark print with a more exact noun. Write the new sentence.

1. Tony and his family visited a **place** in the mountains.

_____

2. Tony took along some boots and warm **clothes**.

_____

3. A fireplace was in one corner of the **room**.

_____

4. The family often sat around the fire and ate **food**.

_____

5. A **person** at a nearby ranch rented Tony a horse.

_____

6. He rode up a steep path to a beautiful **place**.

_____

7. Tony and his dad carried **things** when they went on a hike.

_____

8. They saw several small, furry **animals**.

_____

Common Nouns and Proper Nouns

A **common noun** names any person, place, or thing. It begins with a lowercase letter.
Examples:

inventor   city   month

A **proper noun** names a particular person, place, or thing. Each important word of a proper noun begins with a capital letter.
Examples:

Thomas Alva Edison   Cleveland   August

DIRECTIONS   **Write each noun from the paragraph in the correct box. Capitalize all proper nouns.**

Marcos and his parents are planning a long vacation. They will leave dallas, texas, and drive their car to denver. There they will visit some friends named jackson. Then, they will drive across the western states, through utah and nevada. They hope to see some deer as they drive. Then, the family will spend a week in california. Their cousins live on bay view street in san diego. What an exciting trip that will be!

Common Nouns	**Proper Nouns**
_____	_____
_____	_____
_____	_____
_____	_____
_____	_____
_____	_____
_____	_____
_____	_____

Singular and Plural Nouns

A **singular noun** names one person, one place, or one thing.
Examples:
   dog   house   box
A **plural noun** names more than one person, place, or thing. Make most nouns plural by adding *s* or *es*.
Examples:
   dogs   houses   boxes

DIRECTIONS ➤ Write the plural form of each underlined noun.

1. The <u>kangaroo</u> is native to Australia.

   _____

2. Everyone knows that kangaroos carry their young in a <u>pouch</u>.

   _____

3. A wallaby is a <u>type</u> of small kangaroo.

   _____

4. It isn't the only unusual <u>animal</u> that lives there.

   _____

5. Australia is also the home of a huge bird, the <u>emu</u>.

   _____

6. The emu is only a little smaller than an <u>ostrich</u>.

   _____

7. It eats <u>grass</u>, flowers, insects, and almost anything else.

   _____

8. One very strange <u>mammal</u> from Australia is the platypus.

   _____

9. It looks like a combination of a beaver, a duck, and an <u>otter</u>.

   _____

10. Australia's flying <u>fox</u> is not really a fox at all, but a kind of bat.

    _____

Singular and Plural Nouns, page 2

Remember, a singular noun names one person, place, or thing.
Examples:
    explorer   marsh   sky   monkey
A plural noun names more than one person, place, or thing. Make most nouns plural by adding *s* or *es*. For some nouns ending in *y*, replace the *y* with an *i* and add *es* to form the plural.
Examples:
    explorers   marshes   skies   monkeys

DIRECTIONS ▷ **Rewrite each sentence by giving the plural form of each noun in ( ).**

1. Many (animal) travel in groups.

   _____

2. Monarch (butterfly) travel in swarms of a million or more.

   _____

3. Each year these (insect) migrate.

   _____

4. Many (bird) also travel in groups.

   _____

5. Each autumn, birds flying south for the winter are heard in the (sky).

   _____

6. Canadian geese are famous for their long yearly (journey).

   _____

7. Many fish hatch in (river).

   _____

8. Even people who live in (city) can see migrating animals.

   _____

Special Plural Nouns

Some nouns change their spelling in the plural forms.
Other nouns have the same singular and plural forms.
Examples:

Change Spelling	Same Singular and Plural
man–men	salmon
child–children	elk
foot–feet	deer
goose–geese	trout
wolf–wolves	sheep

◎◎◎ ◎◎ ◎◎ ◎◎◎ ◎◎ ◎◎ ◎◎ ◎◎◎ ◎◎◎ ◎◎◎ ◎◎ ◎◎ ◎◎◎ ◎◎◎ ◎◎ ◎◎ ◎◎ ◎

DIRECTIONS **Write the plural form of the noun in ( ).**

1. The kindergarten _____ put on a health and safety play for the
   (child)
   rest of the school.

2. The play was written by two _____ whose children are in
   (man)
   the class.

3. A girl in blue _____ played the part of a police officer.
   (pants)

4. The clown wore huge shoes on his _____.
   (foot)

5. Three girls dressed as _____ explained why people should wear
   (mouse)
   seat belts.

6. Two _____ recited a poem about bicycle safety.
   (goose)

7. Several of the boys were dressed as _____.
   (sheep)

8. They told a group of _____ how to be safe while swimming.
   (deer)

9 The boys dressed as _____ were the stars of the show.
   (moose)

10. They sang a song about how to brush _____.
    (tooth)

◎◎◎ ◎◎ ◎◎ ◎◎◎ ◎◎ ◎◎ ◎◎ ◎◎◎ ◎◎◎ ◎◎◎ ◎◎ ◎◎ ◎◎◎ ◎◎◎ ◎◎ ◎◎ ◎◎ ◎

Singular Possessive Nouns

A **singular possessive noun** shows ownership by one person or thing. Add an apostrophe (') and *s* to most singular nouns to show possession.
Examples:

Satoh's dog   the dog's teeth

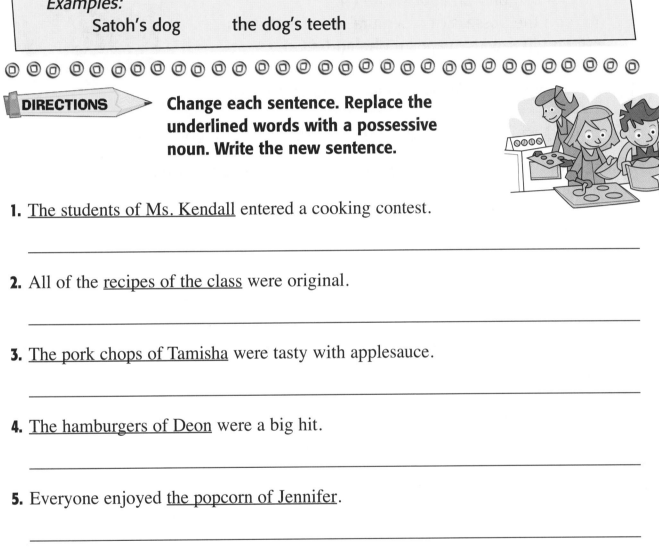

DIRECTIONS ▷ Change each sentence. Replace the underlined words with a possessive noun. Write the new sentence.

1. The students of Ms. Kendall underlined: <u>The students of Ms. Kendall</u> entered a cooking contest.

_____

2. All of the <u>recipes of the class</u> were original.

_____

3. <u>The pork chops of Tamisha</u> were tasty with applesauce.

_____

4. <u>The hamburgers of Deon</u> were a big hit.

_____

5. Everyone enjoyed <u>the popcorn of Jennifer</u>.

_____

6. The <u>flavor of the popcorn</u> was very spicy.

_____

7. <u>The pizza of Mario</u> won the grand prize.

_____

8. The <u>topping of the pizza</u> was made of fresh vegetables.

_____

Plural Possessive Nouns

A **plural possessive noun** shows ownership by more than one person or thing.
To form the possessive of a plural noun ending in *s* or *es*, add only an apostrophe (').
To form the possessive of a plural noun that does not end in *s*, add an apostrophe and *s* ('s).
Examples:

cars' tires   foxes' home   children's books

DIRECTIONS   Write each group of words in the possessive form.

1. the clothes of the scarecrows

_____

2. the smiles of the pumpkins

_____

3. the hats of the sisters

_____

4. the flavor of the seeds

_____

5. the stems of the plants

_____

6. the costumes of the women

_____

7. the colors of the flowers

_____

8. the shapes of the leaves

_____

9. the games of the children

_____

10. the calves of the moose

_____

11. the wool of the sheep

_____

12. the teachers of the classes

_____

13. the toys of the babies

_____

14. the sounds of the drums

_____

Pronouns

A **pronoun** is a word that takes the place of one or more nouns.
Use pronouns to avoid repeating words.
A **singular pronoun** replaces a singular noun. The words *I, me, you, he, she, him, her,* and *it* are singular pronouns. Always capitalize the pronoun *I.*
A **plural pronoun** replaces a plural noun. The words *we, you, they, us,* and *them* are plural pronouns.
Examples:
    The traveler thought *he* should go to the city.
    He takes the place of *the traveler.*
    The campers searched for a place *they* could spend the night.
    They takes the place of *the campers.*

DIRECTIONS Circle the pronoun in the second sentence of each pair. Write the noun or nouns it replaced.

1. Tornadoes are frightening storms. They are strong, whirling winds.

_____

2. The funnel reaches down from dark clouds. It may strike Earth.

_____

3. Scientists are studying tornadoes. Exactly why the storms develop is a mystery to them.

_____

4. Kayla watched a tornado strike near her town. "I was afraid of that swirling funnel."

_____

5. The storm didn't hurt Kayla. She was too far away.

_____

6. Grandpa has an underground shelter in the backyard. He calls the shelter a storm cellar.

_____

7. During "tornado weather," Grandpa watches the sky and listens to the radio. Grandma tells him to be careful.

_____

8. Grandpa calls Phil and Brian if a tornado is coming. "You must stay in the cellar until the storm is over."

_____

Pronouns, page 2

Remember, a pronoun is a word that takes the place of one or more nouns.

Use pronouns to avoid repeating words.

A singular pronoun replaces a singular noun. The words *I, me, you, he, she, him, her,* and *it* are singular pronouns. Always capitalize the pronoun *I.*

A plural pronoun replaces a plural noun. The words *we, you, they, us,* and *them* are plural pronouns.

DIRECTIONS Read each sentence. Write the pronoun or pronouns in each sentence on the line.

1. Robin and Paul's garden has many weeds in it.

_____

2. The two of them grow plants.

_____

3. She reads about weeds.

_____

4. He searches through plant catalogs for odd fruits and vegetables.

_____

5. They try to grow them in the garden.

_____

6. "We grow many things," Robin said.

_____

7. "A friend helped us plant popcorn last spring," Paul said.

_____

8. "I will let you try the popcorn later in the afternoon," he said to me.

_____

9. "What are they?" I asked.

_____

10. "They are oxeye daisies, the prettiest weeds in the garden!" she said.

_____

Subject Pronouns

A **subject pronoun** takes the place of one or more nouns in the subject of a sentence. The words *I*, *you, he, she, it, we,* and *they* are subject pronouns.
Examples:

He brought a spider to school.
We do not like spiders.
You can hold the spider.

> **DIRECTIONS** → Read the paragraph below. Circle all the subject pronouns. Write the circled subject pronouns in the first column below. Then, write the word or words each pronoun replaces.

Sequoia was a member of the Cherokee nation. Sequoia developed a written alphabet for his people. He is also remembered because of the trees that bear his name. Sequoia trees are some of the largest and oldest living things on Earth. They can live for several thousand years! The General Sherman Tree in Sequoia National Park is one of the world's tallest trees. It is 272.4 feet tall.

Subject Pronoun	Word or Words It Replaces
_____	_____
_____	_____
_____	_____

> **DIRECTIONS** → Imagine that you are a scientist studying sequoia trees. Write a few sentences that you might include in your field notes. Use at least three subject pronouns.

_____

_____

_____

Object Pronouns

An **object pronoun** follows an action verb, such as *see* or *tell*, or a word such as *about, at, for, from, near, of, to,* or *with*.
The words *me, you, him, her, it, us,* and *them* are object pronouns.
Examples:
> Chan took *it* home.
> Dad had a letter for *me*.
> My sister heard *you*.

DIRECTIONS ➤ Rewrite each sentence. Replace the underlined words with pronouns.

1. Emilia and Miguel visited the zoo with <u>their aunt</u>.

_____

2. The zoo seemed strange to <u>Emilia and Miguel</u>.

_____

3. There were no cages in <u>the zoo</u>.

_____

4. "I'll show <u>Miguel and Emilia</u> the giraffes first," their aunt told them.

_____

5. An ostrich wandered right up to <u>their car</u>.

_____

6. "The ostrich wanted a closer look at <u>Miguel and me</u>," Emilia laughed.

_____

7. Monkey Island made a good home for <u>monkeys</u>.

_____

8. Emilia asked <u>Miguel</u> to take a picture of the monkeys.

_____

I, Me, We, Us

Use *I* and *we* as subject pronouns.
Use *me* and *us* as object pronouns.
Examples:

I like to read books.
We have to read two books this month.
Dad took *me* to the library.
The librarian showed *us* the books.

DIRECTIONS — **Write the pronoun in ( ) that correctly completes each sentence.**

1. In science class _____ read a story about penguins.
(we, us)

2. Jill and _____ saw the Falkland Islands on a map.
(I, me)

3. The story told _____ about penguins that live there.
(we, us)

4. Our teacher showed Darrell and _____ a picture of some
(I, me)
rockhopper penguins.

5. _____ learned that they may jump into the ocean instead of
(We, Us)
diving in.

6. They looked funny to my friends and _____.
(I, me)

7. The story told _____ about gentoo penguins.
(we, us)

8. _____ found out that penguins lay eggs in a rookery.
(We, Us)

9. The king penguin looked big to Jill and _____.
(I, me)

10. Tony gave a picture of one to _____.
(we, us)

11. _____ read that the adult king penguin can grow three feet tall.
(I, Me)

Possessive Pronouns

A **possessive pronoun** shows ownership. Some possessive pronouns are *my, your, his, her, its, our,* and *their.*
Examples:
    Skippy is *my* horse.
    He stays in *our* barn.
    Who is *your* pet?

DIRECTIONS ▸ Rewrite each sentence. Replace the underlined words with a possessive pronoun.

1. Jason and Jana visited <u>Abraham Lincoln's</u> birthplace.

_____

2. <u>The park's</u> location is near Hodgenville, Kentucky.

_____

3. <u>Lincoln's</u> birthplace was a small, one-room log cabin.

_____

4. <u>Mr. and Mrs. Lincoln's</u> original cabin has been restored.

_____

5. Only a few of <u>the cabin's</u> original logs are left.

_____

6. <u>Jana's</u> climb up the steps to the cabin left her out of breath.

_____

7. "May I use <u>Jana's</u> camera?" Jason asked Jana.

_____

8. <u>Lincoln's</u> cabin is now part of a beautiful park.

_____

Contractions with Pronouns

> A **contraction** is a short way of writing two words together. Some of the letters are left out. An apostrophe (') takes the place of the missing letters.
>
> Form some contractions by joining pronouns and verbs.
>
> *Examples:*
>
> I + would = *I'd*
> you + are = *you're*
> it + is = *it's*

◎ ◎◎ ◎◎ ◎◎◎ ◎◎ ◎◎ ◎◎ ◎◎ ◎◎ ◎◎◎ ◎◎ ◎◎ ◎◎ ◎◎ ◎◎ ◎◎ ◎◎

DIRECTIONS ➤ **Replace the underlined words with a contraction.**

1. <u>I would</u> _____ like to visit the National Air and Space Museum in Washington, D.C.

2. <u>It is</u> _____ full of exhibits of flying machines.

3. <u>I am</u> _____ going there next June with my uncle.

4. <u>He is</u> _____ a pilot in the Air Force.

5. <u>We are</u> _____ going to see all 20 galleries of the museum.

6. <u>I will</u> _____ ask Uncle Roy to show me the Wright brothers' plane.

7. <u>He has</u> _____ seen it several times.

8. "<u>You will</u> _____ think their plane looks really small," Uncle Roy wrote to me.

9. "<u>We will</u> _____ see several spacecraft, too."

10. It's hard to believe <u>they have</u> _____ really been into space.

11. <u>They are</u> _____ part of an exciting exhibit about space flight.

12. At the museum <u>you are</u> _____ even able to see a rock from the moon.

◎ ◎◎◎◎◎◎◎ ◎◎◎◎◎ ◎◎◎ ◎◎◎ ◎Pronouns◎◎◎ ◎◎◎ ◎◎

Adjectives

An **adjective** is a word that describes a noun or pronoun. Adjectives can tell how many, what color, or what size or shape. They can also describe how something feels, sounds, tastes, or smells.
Use exact adjectives to paint clear word pictures.
Examples:

　　Two birds were in the nest.
　　The *blue* ball was in a *big* box.
　　The *smooth* soap has a *sweet* smell.

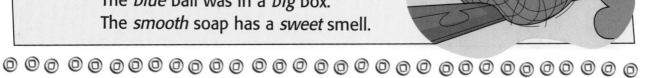

DIRECTIONS ▷ **Read the following paragraph. Underline each adjective.**

The seven families checked the wagons carefully. Were the leather harnesses ready? Two strong oxen would pull each wagon, and many families were bringing several extra oxen. Tomorrow would be the first day of the long journey on the Oregon Trail. In six months, each family would be in a new home in the West.

DIRECTIONS ▷ **Complete the sentences. Write a different adjective on each line.**

1. The children felt _____ about the _____ trip.

2. They expected to see _____ animals, _____ trees, and _____ flowers.

3. Their parents worried about traveling over _____ mountains and through _____, _____ deserts.

4. Families felt _____ about leaving their _____ friends behind.

More Adjectives

Remember to use an adjective to describe a noun or a pronoun.
Use adjectives to give clear and vivid pictures.
Examples:

      Cold lemonade tasted good after the *spicy* food.
      I cuddled up by the *blazing* fire on a *starless* night.

DIRECTIONS ▸ **Write a vivid adjective to complete each sentence.**

1. Kerry has a _____ puppy named Button.

2. Button was born on a _____ night in February.

3. Kerry loves to stroke the dog's _____ fur.

4. Button's _____ ways make him fun to watch.

5. He leaps high into the air, chasing _____ butterflies.

6. He may fall on his chin when he tries to run with his _____ legs.

7. Button's favorite game is playing school in Kerry's _____ playhouse.

8. He chews on a _____ shoe while Kerry pretends to be the teacher.

9. When the weather is warm, Button naps under a _____ tree.

10. At night Kerry tucks him into a _____ basket.

11. "His _____ ears make him so cute," Kerry says.

12. "Nobody could resist those _____ eyes, either."

Predicate Adjectives

An adjective is a word that describes a noun or pronoun. A **predicate adjective** follows a linking verb such as *is, seems,* or *looks.* When an adjective follows a linking verb, it can describe the subject of the sentence. *Examples:*

> That elephant is *huge.*
>
> That snake looks *scary.*

 **DIRECTIONS** > Circle each adjective that follows the linking verb. Then, underline the noun or pronoun it describes.

1. Our zoo's old cages were small and dark.

2. A visitor to the zoo was unhappy about this.

3. He was sorry for the animals.

4. Now, new homes for the animals are large and airy.

5. The animals are content in their new zoo homes.

DIRECTIONS > Write adjectives to complete each sentence. Underline the noun or pronoun each adjective describes.

6. The zoo's elephant is _____, _____, and
   _____.

7. Its ears are _____ and _____.

8. Its zoo home is _____ and _____.

9. The nearby monkeys are _____, _____, and
   _____.

10. During the daytime, they are _____ and _____.

Articles

The words *a*, *an*, and *the* are called **articles**.
Use *a* before a word that begins with a consonant sound.
Use *an* before a word that begins with a vowel sound.
Use *the* before a word that begins with a consonant or a vowel.
Examples:

  Have you ever seen *an* owl?
  The owl is *a* nocturnal animal.

DIRECTIONS → **Write the article in ( ) that correctly completes each sentence.**

1. Pete wants to be _____ (a, an) sportswriter for

_____ (a, an) newspaper when he grows up.

2. Now he writes stories for _____ (an, the) school paper.

3. "Covering baseball games is _____ (a, the) most fun," Pete says.

4. "Last week I wrote about _____ (a, an) tennis match, too."

5. His teacher says that Pete is _____ (a, an) excellent writer.

6. "His stories make _____ (a, the) readers feel as if they are

watching the game," the teacher says.

7. Pete's mother is _____ (a, an) English teacher.

8. Sometimes she helps him find just _____ (an, the) right words to

use in _____ (a, an) story.

9. It may take him _____ (a, an) hour to write one story.

10. "Sports writing is _____ (a, an) exciting job," says Pete.

11. "It's fun to have _____ (a, an) interview with

_____ (a, an) player."

12. When Pete is _____ (a, an) adult, he would like to work for

_____ (an, the) *New York Times*.

Adjectives That Compare: *er, est*

Add *er* to most short adjectives to compare two nouns or pronouns.
Add *est* to most short adjectives to compare more than two nouns or
pronouns.
Change the *y* to *i* before adding *er* or *est* to adjectives that end in a
consonant and *y*.
Example:
This building is *taller* than that one.
My hair is *curlier* than yours.
The whale is the *largest* of all animals.

DIRECTIONS Write the correct form of the adjective in ( ) to complete each sentence.

1. Yellowstone is the _____ of all our national parks.
(old)

2. It is 18 years _____ than Yosemite National Park.
(old)

3. Tracy thinks it is _____ than Yosemite, too.
(pretty)

4. "Yellowstone has the _____ scenery I've ever seen," Tracy said.
(strange)

5. Great Fountain Geyser sometimes shoots water _____ than a
(high)
20-story building.

6. "I can't imagine anything _____ than a geyser," said Tracy.
(strange)

7. Yellowstone Lake is our country's _____ high-altitude lake.
(large)

8. Its sparkling water seems _____ than a mirror.
(shiny)

9. "It is the _____ lake I've seen," said Tracy.
(smooth)

10. Yellowstone has a deep canyon, but the Grand Canyon in Arizona is

_____.
(deep)

Adjectives That Compare: more, most

Use *more* with some adjectives to compare two nouns or pronouns.
Use *most* with some adjectives to compare more than two nouns or pronouns.
Examples:
Diving may be the *most difficult* of all sports.
It is *more interesting* to watch than golf.

DIRECTIONS Write *more* or *most* to complete each sentence.

1. "Making Kites" was one of the _____ creative classes Jamie had attended.

2. It was _____ fun than the class about clowns.

3. The teacher, Mr. Vargas, was _____ helpful than a textbook.

4. The kites the students made were _____ complex than a simple piece of cloth or plastic.

5. The kite's design took _____ exact measurements than Jamie had expected.

6. Of all the students, Jamie was the _____ careful when he cut out his kite.

7. Mr. Vargas's kite was _____ unusual than Jamie's.

8. It had the _____ remarkable design in the class.

9. Its butterfly shape was _____ difficult to make than Jamie's diamond shape was.

10. Mr. Vargas used the _____ durable kite material he could find.

Special Forms of Adjectives That Compare

Some adjectives have special forms for comparing.
Examples:
Omar has a *good* food puppet.
Chad's puppet is *better* than Omar's.
Teena's celery stalk is the *best* of all the food puppets.

Adjective	Comparing Two Things	Comparing More Than Two Things
good	better	best
bad	worse	worst

DIRECTIONS → **Read each sentence, and circle the correct word in ( ).**

1. Making talking vegetable puppets was the (worstest, worst) idea I ever had.

2. I was much (worse, worst) than my classmates at making puppets.

3. Then, I became (better, gooder) at it.

4. John's carrot looked much (worse, worser) than mine.

5. Suno said her tomato was the (worse, worst) puppet.

6. Her eggplant puppet will look much (better, best).

7. The (best, goodest) puppets are usually not the most realistic.

8. Sasha's new broccoli puppet is (better, best) than his last one because it's brighter.

9. The (bestest, best) part is giving the show.

10. The (worse, worst) part is cleaning up at the end.

Verbs

A **verb** is a word that expresses action or being.
A verb is the main word in the predicate of a sentence. A verb and its subject should agree in number.
Examples:
People all over the world *play* board games.
The game of checkers *is* more than 700 years old.

DIRECTIONS ▸ **Circle the verb in each sentence.**

1. The French probably invented the game of checkers.

2. Most checkerboards have 64 squares.

3. Chinese checkers probably came from Europe.

4. Nine planets revolve around our Sun.

5. Pluto is the planet farthest from the Sun.

6. It circles the Sun every 248 years.

7. Pluto was unknown to scientists 100 years ago.

8. Percival Lowell estimated the location of the planet in 1915.

9. He never found the planet.

10. In 1930, Clyde Tombaugh studied the sky with a powerful telescope.

11. He took many photographs through the telescope.

12. Three of his photographs showed a distant planet.

Action Verbs

An **action verb** is a word that shows action.
An action verb is the main word in the predicate of a sentence. An action verb tells what the subject of a sentence does or did.
Use strong action verbs to paint clear and vivid pictures.
Examples:
> Sandy *ran* along the path.
> She *jumped* over the sleeping dog.

DIRECTIONS ▷ Write an action verb to complete each sentence.

1. Jets at an air show _____ at top speed.

2. First, they _____ along the ground.

3. Then, they _____ into the air like giant birds.

4. Some pilots _____ stunts at air shows.

5. They _____ their planes upside down in the air.

6. Sometimes sky divers _____ from a plane.

7. They _____ to the ground under colorful parachutes.

8. A daring wing-walker _____ on the wing of a flying plane.

9. She _____ the safety rope tightly.

10. Restored antique planes _____ overhead in formation.

11. On the ground, visitors _____ many types of aircraft.

12. People of all ages _____ an air show.

Main Verbs

Sometimes a simple predicate is made up of two or more verbs. The **main verb** is the most important verb in the predicate. It comes last in a group of verbs.
Examples:
People around the world *have <u>played</u>* board games for years.
We *are <u>learning</u>* games from many countries.

DIRECTIONS Read each sentence, and write the main verb on the line.

1. People in India are playing "Snakes and Ladders."

   _____

2. They have made a game board with 100 squares.

   _____

3. They are throwing dice.

   _____

4. Alicia has collected hundreds of coins.

   _____

5. Alicia is sorting the coins in her collection.

   _____

6. She has received a box of pennies.

   _____

7. Alicia's great-grandfather had collected some of the pennies.

   _____

8. He had saved a penny from the year 1794.

   _____

9. Alicia has added many coins to the collection.

   _____

10. She is putting her oldest dime away.

    _____

11. She will display it tomorrow at the hobby show.

    _____

12. She has won a blue ribbon before.

    _____

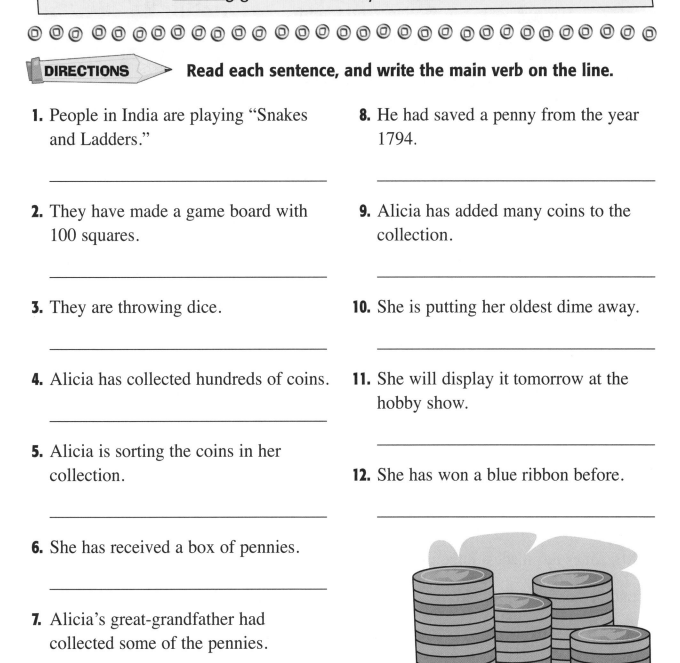

Helping Verbs

A **helping verb** can work with the main verb to tell about an action. The helping verb always comes before the main verb. These words are often used as helping verbs: *am, is, are, was, were, has, have, had,* and *will.* Sometimes another word comes between a main verb and a helping verb.
Examples:
Our class *is* <u>organizing</u> a large picnic.
We *will* <u>invite</u> our families and friends.
The class *will* certainly <u>have</u> a lot to do.

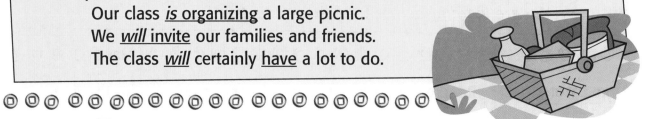

DIRECTIONS → In each sentence, circle the helping verb. Then, write the verb it is helping.

1. Mr. and Mrs. Ames have invited us to their farm.

   _____

2. We are planning a game.

   _____

3. Mrs. Chu is helping us.

   _____

4. We will play a game of "Mud Tug."

   _____

5. Mr. Ames has made a huge mud puddle near the cornfield.

   _____

6. Two teams will tug on a rope.

   _____

7. One unlucky team will probably fall into the mud.

   _____

8. At first Mrs. Chu had said no to "Mud Tug."

   _____

9. She had worried about the mess.

   _____

10. Everyone will bring a change of clothes.

    _____

Main and Helping Verbs

Remember that the main verb is the most important verb in a sentence. The helping verb works with the main verb to tell about an action. A helping verb often shows when the action in a sentence happens.

 **DIRECTIONS** **Read the paragraph below. Circle each helping verb. Then, underline the main verb.**

I am reading a book called Planet 945. My brother has read it, too! In the book, some pioneers are settling a new planet. No one has explored the planet yet, so they will have some amazing adventures there. In Chapter 4, two children are looking for a lost dog. They have discovered a ruined city.

DIRECTIONS **Complete each sentence with a helping verb.**

1. Kim and Ho _____ searching for the lost dog.

2. Kim _____ spotted a gleam between two hills.

3. "I _____ tired," Ho said.

4. "I _____ head for that valley," answered Kim. "You can rest here."

5. Ho _____ napping under a bush when Kim came back.

6. "Come and see. I _____ found the ruins of an old city!" she cried.

DIRECTIONS **Write two sentences about a weird encounter. Use a helping verb in each sentence.**

_____

_____

Linking Verbs

A **linking verb** connects the subject to a word or words in the predicate. The most common linking verbs are forms of *be*. Some forms of *be* are *am*, *is*, *are*, *was*, and *were.* Use *am, is,* and *are* to show present tense. Use *was* and *were* to show past tense. Some other common linking verbs are *become, feel,* and *seem.*
Examples:

> Duane and Aisha *are* in the backyard.
> They *seem* happy about something.

DIRECTIONS → Write a linking verb to complete each sentence.

1. One of my favorite novels _____ Caddie Woodlawn.

2. It _____ a book by Carol Ryrie Brink.

3. Caddie, a lively young girl, _____ the main character.

4. She and her family _____ pioneers in Wisconsin in the 1860s.

5. Caddie's life _____ full of adventure.

6. In those days, girls _____ expected to be quiet and stay indoors most of the time.

7. I _____ sure Caddie didn't like to cook and sew all the time.

8. She _____ happiest when she was outdoors, running and playing with her brothers.

9. Caddie's neighbors _____ afraid of the Native Americans who lived across the river.

10. Caddie _____ a friend of theirs.

11. She _____ able to prove that all the people could be friends.

12. I _____ glad that I took the time to read the book.

Action Verbs and Linking Verbs

Remember, verbs that tell what the subject of a sentence does or did are action verbs. Verbs that tell what the subject of a sentence is or is like are called linking verbs.

◎ ◎

> **DIRECTIONS** — **Read the paragraph below. Circle each action verb. Underline each linking verb.**

Last summer my friends and I invented a game called "Quick Changes." In this game we write the names of real or imaginary creatures on slips of paper. Each player takes a slip. For ten minutes, each player is the animal on the slip. For example, I was a seal one morning. I flopped around in the wading pool. I barked. I splashed water at my friends.

> **DIRECTIONS** — **Use a form of the linking verb *be* to complete each sentence.**

1. José and I _____ eager to play the new game.

2. "Oh, boy! I _____ an eagle!" says José.

3. "_____ you ready for your turn?" asks Sara.

4. Maria _____ a bat, hanging from a tree branch.

5. Some of my friends _____ really silly.

6. "This _____ a very strange game!" says José's sister.

> **DIRECTIONS** — **Write two sentences about a game you and your friends enjoy. Use at least one action verb and one linking verb.**

_____

_____

Present-Tense Verbs

A **present-tense verb** tells about actions that are happening now.
Add *s* or *es* to most present-tense verbs when the subject of the
sentence is *he, she, it,* or a singular noun.
Do not add *s* or *es* to a present-tense verb when the
subject is *I, you, we, they,* or a plural noun.
Examples:
   Maria's family *grows* coffee beans.
   She *watches* the harvest.
   The beans *grow* on bushes.

DIRECTIONS ▷ **Write the present-tense form of the verb in ( ) that correctly completes each sentence.**

1. Dougal Dixon _____ books that stretch the reader's imagination.
(write)

2. In his book <u>The New Dinosaurs</u>, he _____ what dinosaurs might
(imagine)
be like if they were still alive today.

3. Dixon _____ that dinosaurs would have changed very much
(believe)
since ancient times.

4. His ideas _____ science and fiction in an exciting way.
(mix)

5. He _____ pictures of the animals that he imagines.
(draw)

6. The long-haired kloon _____ its feet like hands.
(use)

7. A graceful bird called a soar _____ in the ocean with its
(fish)
long neck.

8. The seal-like plunger _____ fish with its sharp teeth.
(crush)

9. The neck of the lank _____ high into the air like a giraffe's.
(reach)

10. The harridan _____ with wings that fold up when it walks.
(fly)

Past-Tense Verbs

A **past-tense verb** tells about actions that happened in the past.
Add *ed* or *d* to most present-tense verbs to make them show past tense.
You may have to drop an *e*, double a final consonant, or change a *y* to an *i*.
Examples:
> Long ago, hunters *hunted* huge mammoths.
> These gigantic mammoths *died* long ago.

DIRECTIONS ▷ **Write the past-tense form of the verb in ( ).**

1. When Mr. King was a boy, he _____ on a farm.
   (live)

2. He and his sisters _____ more than three miles to school.
   (hike)

3. They always _____ their lunches.
   (carry)

4. "When we were thirsty, we _____ water from a nearby spring,"
   (dip)

   Mr. King said.

5. "There were no school cafeterias in those days," he _____.
   (observe)

6. When Mr. King finished high school, he _____ to the city.
   (move)

7. He _____ to become a teacher.
   (study)

8. "Even when I began teaching, students still _____ their own
   (provide)

   lunches," Mr. King told us.

9. In about 1940, the "bring your lunch" system _____.
   (change)

10. People _____ because many children were coming to school with
    (worry)

    nothing to eat.

11. The government _____ food and money for the schools to use to
    (supply)

    serve hot lunches.

Future-Tense Verbs

A **future-tense verb** shows action that will happen in the future.
To form the future tense of a verb, use the helping verb *will* with the main verb.

Examples:

Tomorrow we *will visit* my aunt's new restaurant.
The cook *will make* my favorite tamales for dinner.

DIRECTIONS → Circle the future-tense verb in ( ) to complete each sentence.

1. First, the cook (will steam / steamed) the corn meal.

2. Then, he (chop / will chop) some chicken into pieces.

3. His assistant (will mix / mix) it with herbs and spices.

4. Finally, he (will put / had put) the tamales together.

5. We (will have / having) frijoles, too.

6. Our tour of Parker Ranch (will stretch / stretch) across many miles of the big island of Hawaii.

7. We (learned / will learn) about the history of ranching in the Hawaiian Islands.

8. In the afternoon, we (listening / will listen) to a talk about King Kamehameha the Great.

9. We (will see / saw) the remains of the king's home at Kailua tomorrow morning.

10. After that we (will head / heads) home.

Future-Tense Verbs, page 2

Remember that a future-tense verb shows action that will happen in the future. To form the future tense of a verb, use the helping verb *will* with the main verb.

DIRECTIONS ▷ **Rewrite each sentence. Change the verb to the future tense.**

1. A blanket of cold air settles on the valley.

   _____

2. Ms. Asato reads the weather data on her computer.

   _____

3. She records a warning on an answering machine.

   _____

4. Hundreds of fruit and nut growers call the line.

   _____

5. Frost damages young plants and buds on trees.

   _____

6. The growers work late into the night.

   _____

7. They roll their huge wind machines into the orchards.

   _____

8. These giant fans move the air.

   _____

9. The movement of the air raises temperatures a few degrees.

   _____

10. Wet ground also keeps temperatures higher.

    _____

Irregular Verbs

An **irregular verb** is a verb that does not end with *ed* to show past tense. Some irregular verbs show past tense by using a different form of the main verb with *have, has,* or *had.*
Examples:

Present	Past	Past with Helping Verb
do, does	did	(have, has, had) done
come, comes	came	(have, has, had) come
run, runs	ran	(have, has, had) run
go, goes	went	(have, has, had) gone

DIRECTIONS ▷ **Write the correct past-tense form of the verb in ( ).**

1. Last summer Kara _____ on an exciting raft ride.
(go)

2. She had _____ on several rafting trips before.
(go)

3. She never had _____ a river as swift as this one.
(see)

4. The trip _____ just above a deep canyon.
(begin)

5. "We _____ it would be fun to ride the rapids through the
(think)
canyon," Kara explained.

6. The leader had _____ a life jacket for each person.
(bring)

7. "The leader _____ we should wear our life jackets at all times,"
(say)
Kara pointed out.

8. "We climbed into the raft, and the wild ride _____."
(begin)

9. Excitement _____ Kara's heart pound as the raft plunged through
(make)
the roaring rapids.

10. "The trip was a little scary, but I was glad I _____."
(go)

More Irregular Verbs

Remember that an irregular verb is a verb that does not end with *ed* to show past tense. Some irregular verbs use *n* or *en* when they are combined with *have, has,* or *had.*

DIRECTIONS **Add words to complete each sentence. Use the correct form of the verb in ( ).**

1. The wind has _____.
(blow)

2. All the leaves have _____.
(fall)

3. My kite _____.
(fly)

4. A shower of acorns _____.
(fall)

5. A busy squirrel _____.
(dig)

6. In the garden, pumpkins have _____.
(grow)

7. Yesterday my friend and I _____.
(ride)

8. We have _____.
(ride)

9. My brother _____.
(write)

10. He has _____.
(write)

11. Our neighbor had _____.
(give)

12. Mom and Dad have _____.
(speak)

Adverbs

An **adverb** is a word that describes a verb.

An adverb may tell how, when, or where an action happens. Many adverbs that tell how end in *ly*.

Vary your sentences by moving the adverbs.

Examples:

Today we visited a zoo.

We walked through *there slowly*.

DIRECTIONS Rewrite each sentence to include the adverb in ( ).

1. Kristen visited the Science Museum. (yesterday)

_____

2. She saw an exhibit of holograms. (upstairs)

_____

3. She tried to touch the images. (first)

_____

4. She learned why holograms look so real. (finally)

_____

5. Kristen will go again. (there)

_____

DIRECTIONS Complete each sentence with an adverb that tells when or where.

6. Look at the fossil exhibit _____.
(When?)

7. Mammoth bones are displayed _____.
(Where?)

8. The exhibit opened _____.
(When?)

9. _____ it will close.
(When?)

More Adverbs

Remember that an adverb is a word that describes a verb. Some adverbs tell *how* about a verb. Many adverbs that tell how end in *ly*.

Use adverbs to make sentences more vivid and exact.

Examples:

My mother laughed *loudly*.

We ran *quickly* to the shore.

DIRECTIONS ▷ Rewrite each sentence. Add an adverb from the box to each sentence to make it more vivid.

patiently	quickly	impatiently	carefully
calmly	eagerly	tirelessly	surprisingly
promptly	fast	clumsily	enthusiastically

1. Jeff prepared to go snorkeling for the first time.

_____

2. He strapped on his face mask.

_____

3. "You are learning," the instructor said.

_____

4. Jeff plodded across the beach in his fins.

_____

5. He looked through his mask into an underwater world.

_____

6. Brightly colored fish swam in front of his eyes.

_____

7. Jeff snorkeled for several hours.

_____

Adverbs That Compare

To make some one-syllable adverbs show comparison, add *er* or *est*.
To make adverbs that end in *ly* show comparison, use *more* or *most*.
Examples:

Antonio ran *faster* than anyone else did.

I read *more slowly* than my sister does.

DIRECTIONS Write the correct form of the adverb in ( ).

1. Eric and his friends hiked _____ on the steep trail
(more slowly, most slowly)

than on the flat trail.

2. Of all their camping trips, they had planned

this one _____.
(more carefully, most carefully)

3. At first, the trail climbed

_____ upward.
(steadily, most steadily)

4. The group walked _____ in the morning than
(faster, fastest)

in the afternoon.

5. When they reached the camp, John set his backpack down

_____ than Mike did.
(more eagerly, most eagerly)

6. Eric cooked _____ over the campfire than John did.
(more skillfully, most skillfully)

7. Mike cooked _____ of all.
(more skillfully, most skillfully)

8. Steve could set up a tent _____ than Mike could.
(more quickly, most quickly)

9. Eric worked _____ of all the boys.
(more cheerfully, most cheerfully)

10. He _____ accepted the "Outstanding Camper" award.
(proudly, more proudly)

Adverb or Adjective?

Use an adverb to describe a verb. Use an adjective to describe a noun or pronoun.

○ ○○ ○ ○○ ○○○ ○ ○○ ○ ○ ○ ○○○ ○○○ ○○○ ○○ ○ ○○○ ○ ○○ ○ ○○ ○ ○

DIRECTIONS ▷ **Rewrite each sentence, adding the word in ( ). Write *adverb* or *adjective* to identify the word you added.**

1. <u>Ben and Me</u> is a book about Benjamin Franklin.

(humorous) _____

_____

2. The story is told from a mouse's point of view.

(amusingly) _____

_____

3. <u>Johnny Tremain</u> is another story about early America.

(popular) _____

_____

4. It tells about events of the American Revolution.

(exciting) _____

_____

5. Johnny is a silversmith.

(young) _____

_____

6. He helps the patriots fight for independence.

(willingly) _____

_____

Good and Well

Students often have trouble with *good* and *well*.
Use *good* as an adjective.
Use *well* most often as an adverb.
Examples:
> Britney did a *good* job on her report.
> She writes *well*.

DIRECTIONS Read each sentence. If *good* or *well* is used correctly, write *correct*. If not, write the sentence correctly.

1. Lake Slo was a well fishing spot.

_____

2. It is a good spot if you're a fish!

_____

3. None of the six of us had well luck.

_____

4. I thought I'd do good because I had my best flies.

_____

5. "What good flies!" said Aunt Sendra.

_____

6. "How did you do that so good?"

_____

7. "Dad taught me to use good materials," I replied.

_____

8. It's not a well idea to be in the hot sun all day without a hat.

_____

9. The hot dogs we ate for dinner were good.

_____

What Is a Sentence?

A **sentence** is a group of words that tells a complete thought.
The words in the sentence should be in an order that makes sense.
Begin every sentence with a capital letter, and end it with the correct
end mark.
Examples:
  Cindi's cat has white hair.
  Raoul drew pictures of many animals.

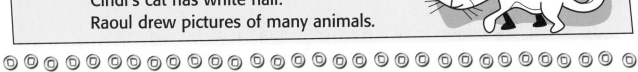

 **DIRECTIONS** Read each word group. Write *sentence* if the word group is a sentence. For each word group that is not a sentence, add words to make it a sentence. Then, write the sentence.

1. Sara saw an unusual animal last summer.

_____

2. In an aquarium in Florida.

_____

3. A worker explained that the huge brown animal was a manatee.

_____

4. Manatees live in water, but they are not fish.

_____

5. Looked somewhat like a big, overgrown seal.

_____

6. Seemed to be tame and friendly.

_____

7. Sara watched the manatee take a whole head of lettuce from the worker's hand.

_____

8. Gobbled up the lettuce with a quick gulp.

_____

Parts of a Sentence

A **sentence** is a group of words that expresses a complete thought. Every sentence has two parts. The **subject** is the part about which something is said. The **predicate** tells about the subject.

Subject	Predicate
Multiplication tables	are learned by students.

The **complete subject** is all the words that make up the subject.
My arithmetic homework was not very easy.

The **simple subject** is the key word or words in the complete subject.
The hardest problems had multiplication.

The **complete predicate** is all the words that tell something about the complete subject.
The science class learned how clouds are formed.

The **simple predicate** is the key word or words in the predicate. The simple predicate is an action verb or linking verb together with any helping verbs.
This geography book describes lakes and rivers.

DIRECTIONS Complete each sentence with a complete subject or a complete predicate.

1. A notebook _____.

2. _____ shows your teacher what you have learned.

3. _____ is the study of countries and people.

4. Language _____.

5. A sentence _____.

Subjects and Predicates

Remember that every sentence has a subject that names the person or thing the sentence is about.

Every sentence has a predicate that tells what the subject of the sentence is or does.

DIRECTIONS **Write the complete subject of each sentence on the lines below. Underline the complete predicate.**

1. Sylvie Martin hears the rain on the roof.

_____

2. The rain is falling softly.

_____

3. The young woman puts on her rain jacket.

_____

4. Her shoes are waterproof.

_____

5. This person walks toward the beach.

_____

6. The streets are quiet today.

_____

7. Sylvie steps carefully over puddles.

_____

8. She hums softly to herself.

_____

9. Her rain jacket keeps her dry.

_____

10. Miss Martin is comfortable in the rain.

_____

Simple Subjects and Complete Subjects

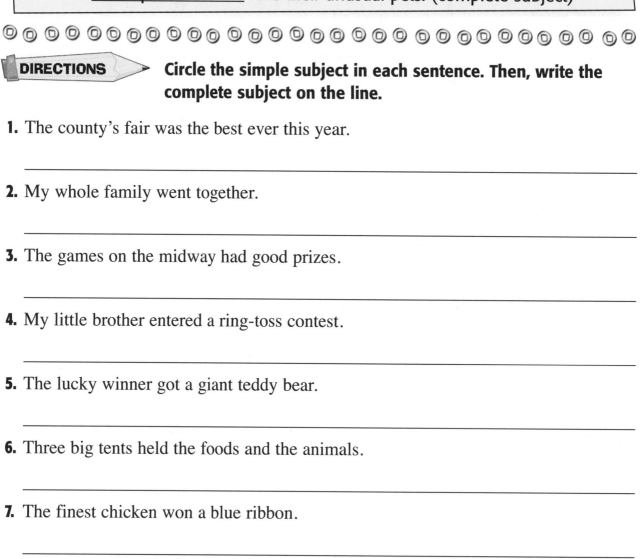

The **simple subject** is the main word or words in the complete subject of a sentence.
The **complete subject** includes all the words that tell whom or what the sentence is about.
Examples:

Many farm <u>children</u> raise pigs for fun. (simple subject)
<u>These proud owners</u> love their unusual pets. (complete subject)

DIRECTIONS ➤ Circle the simple subject in each sentence. Then, write the complete subject on the line.

1. The county's fair was the best ever this year.

_____

2. My whole family went together.

_____

3. The games on the midway had good prizes.

_____

4. My little brother entered a ring-toss contest.

_____

5. The lucky winner got a giant teddy bear.

_____

6. Three big tents held the foods and the animals.

_____

7. The finest chicken won a blue ribbon.

_____

8. A plump hog won the livestock contest.

_____

Compound Subjects

A **compound subject** is two or more subjects joined by *and* or *or*.
These subjects share the same predicate.
Examples:
A child *or* an adult can ride a bicycle.
Health *and* fitness are concerns of many bike riders.

◎◎◎◎◎◎◎◎◎◎◎◎◎◎◎◎◎◎◎◎◎◎◎◎◎◎◎◎◎◎◎◎◎

> **DIRECTIONS** ⟩ Underline the two simple subjects in each sentence.

1. Sun and sand make Hawaii a popular vacation spot.

2. Residents and tourists jam some of the most famous beaches.

3. Peace and quiet can still be found in some places.

4. Molokai and Lanai are less crowded than some other islands.

5. Gorgeous forests and canyons make Kauai a tourist's paradise.

6. Warm weather and tropical breezes lure visitors to Hawaii all year.

> **DIRECTIONS** ⟩ Write sentences using the words below in compound subjects.

7. (shops, restaurants) _____

_____

8. (family, I) _____

_____

9. (airplanes, ships) _____

_____

10. (seafood, pineapple) _____

_____

Simple, Complete, and Compound Subjects

Remember that the simple subject is the main word or words in the complete subject of a sentence. The complete subject includes all the words that tell whom or what the sentence is about. A compound subject is two or more subjects joined by *and* or *or*.

DIRECTIONS Read the paragraph, and underline the complete subject in each sentence. Then, circle the simple subject. If the sentence has a compound subject, circle both simple subjects.

Dogs and humans have lived together happily for thousands of years. Huge hounds and tiny puppies make great pets. They are good company for their owners. Dogs and their owners enjoy playing and exercising together. Dogs help people in special ways. Specially trained dogs work with police officers. Guide dogs lead blind people. Sled dogs can pull heavy loads through the snow. Most dogs and their owners become best friends!

DIRECTIONS Read each set of sentences below. Write one new sentence that has a compound subject.

1. German shepherds can be excellent watchdogs. Doberman pinschers can be excellent watchdogs.

_____

_____

2. Children often enjoy training dogs. Their parents often enjoy training dogs.

_____

_____

Simple Predicates and Complete Predicates

> The **simple predicate** is the main word or words in the complete predicate of a sentence.
> The **complete predicate** includes all the words that tell what the subject of the sentence is or does.
> To locate the simple predicate, find the key word in the complete predicate.
> *Examples:*
>   A rescue dog <u>wears</u> bells on its collar. (simple predicate)
>   Rescue dogs <u>follow the scent of the lost person</u>. (complete predicate)

DIRECTIONS ▸ **Write a simple predicate to complete each sentence. Then, underline the complete predicate.**

1. Visitors to Alaska _____ some of the most beautiful scenery in America.

2. Tall, snowcapped mountains _____ high into the sky.

3. The tallest mountain in North America _____ in central Alaska.

4. Its Native American name, Denali, _____ "the great one."

5. The mountain's official name _____ Mount McKinley.

6. Deep forests _____ much of Alaska.

7. Moose, caribou, mountain sheep, and bears _____ in Alaska's back country.

8. Sometimes a hungry moose _____ into town.

9. A moose at the window _____ a funny but scary sight!

10. Many visitors to Alaska _____ fishing in the clear blue lakes and rushing rivers.

Compound Predicates

A **compound predicate** is two or more predicates that have the same subject.
The simple predicates in a compound predicate are usually joined by *and* or *or*.
Examples:
    Bears *chase <u>or</u> injure* sheep sometimes.
    Guards *watch <u>and</u> protect* the flocks.

DIRECTIONS Write the two simple predicates in each sentence.

1. Raccoon cubs curl into a ball and sleep cozily in their den.

_____

2. Their mother stays close by and cares for them.

_____

3. Sea lions float in the water and sleep at the same time.

_____

4. Sea otters anchor themselves to seaweed and float on their backs.

_____

5. A leopard sprawls along a limb and relaxes in a tree.

_____

DIRECTIONS Complete each sentence with a compound predicate. You may add other words besides verbs.

6. Little kittens _____.

7. My baby cousin _____.

8. Bear cubs _____.

9. My new puppy _____.

10. Lions at the zoo _____.

Simple, Complete, and Compound Predicates

Remember that the simple predicate is the main word or words in the complete predicate of a sentence. The complete predicate includes all the words that tell what the subject of the sentence is or does. A compound predicate is two or more predicates that have the same subject.

DIRECTIONS Read the paragraph, and underline the complete predicate in each sentence. Then, circle the simple predicate. If the sentence has a compound predicate, circle each simple predicate.

Everyone worked hard on the class play. We formed committees and made plans. The script committee discussed the play for hours. The committee members wrote and rewrote the script many times. The final script sounded terrific! The costumes committee worked hard, too. These committee members collected old-fashioned shirts for the cast members. I volunteered for the sets committee. We sketched many different ideas. We chose the best sketch and turned it into a set. We hammered, sawed, and painted for many days.

DIRECTIONS Read each set of sentences below. For each set, write one new sentence that has a compound predicate.

1. The actors read the script. The actors memorized their lines.

   _____

2. Everyone in the audience stood up. Everyone in the audience clapped. Everyone in the audience cheered for us.

   _____

   _____

Simple and Compound Sentences

A sentence that expresses only one complete thought is a **simple sentence**. A **compound sentence** is made up of two or more simple sentences joined by a word such as *and, or,* or *but.* These words are called **conjunctions**. Use a comma (,) before a conjunction that joins two sentences.

Examples:

Cheri sent a poem to a writing contest. (simple sentence)

Three judges liked her poem, *but* two judges did not. (compound sentence)

DIRECTIONS > **The following paragraph is written with simple sentences only. Rewrite the paragraph by combining at least three pairs of simple sentences to make compound sentences.**

Eduardo has always loved the circus. Now he is making plans to become a circus performer. He has taken gymnastics classes. His teacher is impressed with Eduardo's skill. Eduardo also belongs to a drama club. He likes performing in all kinds of plays. Comedies are his favorite. Soon Eduardo will have to decide which skills to develop. He may become a circus acrobat. He may decide to become a circus clown.

_____

_____

_____

_____

_____

_____

_____

_____

_____

Simple and Compound Sentences

Declarative and Interrogative Sentences

Use a **declarative sentence** to make a statement. Begin it with a capital letter and end it with a period (.).
Use an **interrogative sentence** to ask a question. Begin it with a capital letter and end it with a question mark (?).
Examples:
> Ricky draws great pictures. (declarative)
> What did Ricky draw today? (interrogative)

 **DIRECTIONS** **Write each sentence so that it begins and ends correctly. Then, write *declarative* or *interrogative* to tell what kind of sentence it is.**

1. did you know that very few people have been attacked by sharks

_____

_____

2. many types of sharks are not very big

_____

3. one kind is only about as long as your hand

_____

4. how can sharks find food in the dark

_____

5. they use their senses of hearing, smell, and sight

_____

6. some sharks will eat anything

_____

7. have you heard that nails, jewels, and even clothing have been found inside sharks' stomachs

_____

_____

Imperative and Exclamatory Sentences

> Use an **imperative sentence** to make a request or give a command. End it with a period (.).
> Use an **exclamatory sentence** to express strong feeling. End it with an exclamation point (!).
> Begin every sentence with a capital letter.
> *Examples:*
> Don't be afraid to try new things. (imperative)
> Watch out for that bus! (exclamatory)

DIRECTIONS → **Write a period or an exclamation point to end each sentence correctly. After each sentence, write *imperative* or *exclamatory* to tell what kind of sentence it is.**

1. Please let me see that magazine article

_____

2. Wow, what a contest the magazine is having

_____

3. Tell me all about it

_____

4. Give me time to read all the rules

_____

5. Oh, it's a poetry contest

_____

6. How much fun it would be to enter

_____

7. Be sure to find out what the prizes are

_____

8. Wow, that's an exciting Grand Prize

_____

9. What a thrill it would be to win a trip to Washington

_____

10. Please help me write a poem about what it means to be a friend

_____

11. Give me some ideas about what to say

_____

12. Oh, I hope our poem wins a prize

_____

Agreement of Subjects and Verbs

The verb of a sentence must agree with the subject in number.
Examples:
The *player hits* the ball.
The other *players chase* after it.

DIRECTIONS ▸ **Write the verb in ( ) that agrees with the subject.**

1. Breakfast _____ a plate of scrambled eggs and sausage.
   (is, are)

2. These foods _____ good on Earth and in space, too.
   (taste, tastes)

3. In fact, astronauts _____ just such meals on the space shuttle.
   (eat, eats)

4. In the early days of the space program, meals _____ not so tasty.
   (was, were)

5. John Glenn _____ unhappy about having to squeeze his food
   (was, were)
   from tubes.

6. Now astronauts' food _____ better.
   (taste, tastes)

7. It _____ easier to eat, too.
   (is, are)

8. Foil pouches _____ a great variety of things to eat.
   (hold, holds)

9. A meal _____ only about half an hour to prepare on the space
   (take, takes)
   shuttle.

10. Astronauts _____ careful to eat well-balanced meals.
    (is, are)

11. Fruits and vegetables _____ popular on board.
    (is, are)

12. I _____ sure I would like to try some space foods.
    (am, is)

Agreement of Subject Pronouns with Verbs

The verb of a sentence must agree with the subject pronoun in number.
Examples:
> *She knows* the answer.
> *We know* that song.
> *I know* how to whistle.
> *You know* the way.

DIRECTIONS ➤ **Write the verb in ( ) that correctly completes each sentence.**

1. He _____ that deserts are very dry places.
   (know, knows)

2. We _____ to find nothing but sand there.
   (expect, expects)

3. We _____ many different animals there after all.
   (find, finds)

4. They _____ Matt.
   (surprise, surprises)

5. He _____ a type of lizard called a Gila monster.
   (watch, watches)

6. It _____ slowly, looking for food.
   (move, moves)

7. I _____ at a roadrunner chasing an insect.
   (laugh, laughs)

8. It _____ right by Tammy.
   (speed, speeds)

9. She _____ to look at desert plants.
   (like, likes)

10. Sometimes they _____ colorful blooms.
    (show, shows)

11. She _____ a huge saguaro cactus.
    (admire, admires)

12. It _____ over 50 feet tall.
    (grow, grows)

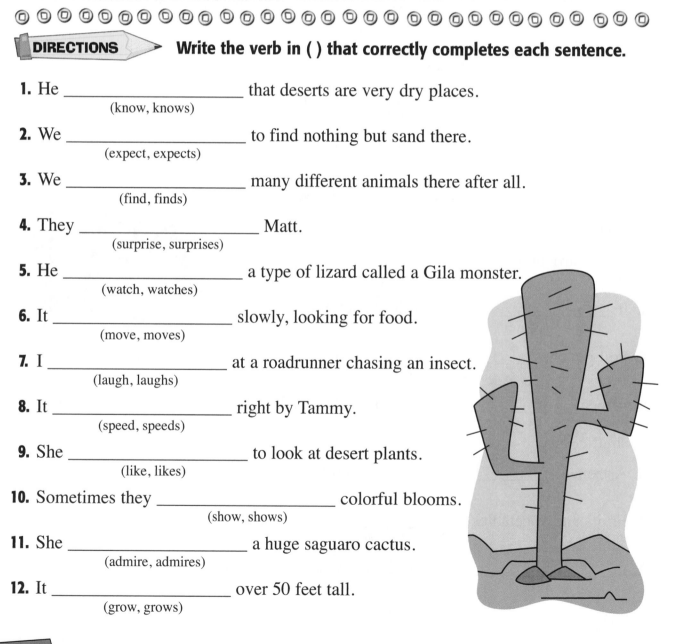

Combining Sentences with the Same Subject

Good writers sometimes combine sentences to make their writing more interesting.

Two short sentences might have the same subject. The writer writes the subject once and then combines the two predicates in the same sentence.
Example:

Bart *liked macaroni.* Bart *liked cheese.*

Bart liked *macaroni and cheese.*

DIRECTIONS **Rewrite the paragraph. Combine pairs of sentences that have the same subjects.**

My parents and I went to Washington, D.C., last year. We left on Monday. We drove for three days. I got tired of riding. I was glad when we arrived in Washington. Dad took us to the Capitol. He showed us our senator's office. Mom loves history. She wanted to see the National Museum of American History. I had read about the pandas. I asked to go to the National Zoo to see them. We all admire Abraham Lincoln. We were thrilled to see the Lincoln Memorial. We had a good time in Washington. We learned a lot about our country, too.

_____

_____

_____

_____

_____

_____

_____

Combining Sentences with the Same Predicate

Good writers often combine short sentences to avoid unnecessary words. Two sentences might have the same predicate. The sentences can be combined by joining the subjects with the word *and*. Be sure that your subjects and verb agree in number.

Example:

Ann likes to play softball. *Trina* likes to play softball.
Ann and Trina like to play softball.

DIRECTIONS ▷ **Combine each pair of sentences to make one sentence. Write the new sentence.**

1. Schools should have ramps as well as steps. Libraries should have ramps as well as steps. _____

_____

2. People in wheelchairs find it hard to climb stairs. People on crutches find it hard to climb stairs. _____

_____

3. Libraries should have elevators. Other public buildings should have elevators.

_____

_____

4. Door handles should be placed low. Elevator buttons should be placed low.

_____

_____

5. People in wheelchairs can reach them there. Everyone else can reach them there.

_____

_____

Joining Sentences

Good writers make their writing more interesting by joining sentences that are short and choppy. Sentences that have ideas that go together can be joined with a comma (,) and the word *and*, *but*, or *or*. Be sure the connecting word makes the meaning of the combined sentences clear.

Example:

Raoul may draw a picture of an elephant.

He may draw a lion instead.

Raoul may draw a picture of an elephant, *or* he may draw a lion instead.

DIRECTIONS ➤ **Join each pair of sentences, and write the new sentences.**

1. Many kinds of spiders spin webs. Not all of the webs are alike.

_____

_____

2. A web may be long and narrow. It may be shaped like a triangle.

_____

_____

3. Some webs are like funnels. Others look more like domes.

_____

_____

4. Wolf spiders hide in burrows. Lynx spiders live on trees or bushes.

_____

_____

5. Many lynx spiders are green. They are hard to find on green leaves.

_____

_____

6. Tarantulas are furry. They look fierce.

_____

Joining Sentences to List Words in a Series

A list of three or more materials or items is called a **series**. Short, choppy sentences can be combined into one long, clear sentence with a series.
Example:

Pet mice can be *black.* They can be *red or silver.*
Pet mice can be *black, red, or silver.*

DIRECTIONS Join each pair of sentences. Write the new sentence.

1. Rey-Ling gave a party. Karen gave a party. Mitch gave a party.

   _____

2. They met on Monday to plan the party. They met on Tuesday and Wednesday to plan the party.

   _____

   _____

3. They invited Tina. They invited Mark. They invited Lee.

   _____

4. Each guest received a paper hat. Each guest received a balloon. Each guest received a new pencil.

   _____

   _____

5. The children played Simon Says. The children played Musical Chairs. The children played Pin the Nose on the Clown.

   _____

   _____

6. Mitch taught the others a new game. Rey-Ling and Karen taught the others a new game.

   _____

7. Tina sang a funny song. Lee sang a funny song. Karen sang a funny song.

   _____

Expanding Sentences

A writer can expand short sentences by adding exact details. The details should be colorful words that give the reader an exact picture of how something looks, sounds, or tastes. These details can also tell more about how something moves or feels.

Examples:

Americans chose the eagle as their symbol.

Americans *proudly* chose the *bald* eagle as their *national* symbol.

How to Expand Sentences
1. Look for sentences that do not give a clear picture of your idea.
2. Think of describing words that give a more exact picture.
3. Add these words to your sentences.

DIRECTIONS ▷ **Add detail words to these sentences to make them more interesting to read.**

1. The _____ owl has often stood for knowledge.

2. People have thought that the bird's _____ eyes showed wisdom.

3. The _____ bear was a symbol for many warriors.

4. These warriors _____ carried their symbol into battle.

5. The _____ Chinese dragon is another symbol.

6. People often think of the _____ koala bear as the symbol for Australia.

7. This _____ animal is not on Australia's coat of arms.

8. Peace is often symbolized by a _____ dove.

9. Many _____ teams use animals as their mascots.

10. A person wears a costume at _____ games.

Avoiding Sentence Fragments and Run-on Sentences

To avoid writing sentence fragments, make sure each sentence has a subject and a predicate and expresses a complete thought.

To avoid writing run-on sentences, be sure you join two complete sentences with a comma and a linking word. You may also write them as two separate sentences.

DIRECTIONS ▷ Rewrite each sentence fragment and run-on sentence. Add words to make the fragments into complete sentences. Change each run-on sentence into a compound sentence or two simple sentences.

1. I went to see a play it was based on the book <u>Charlotte's Web</u>.

_____

_____

2. No adult actors.

_____

3. Played the part of Wilbur the pig.

_____

4. Charlotte was a very smart spider Wilbur was her friend.

_____

_____

5. Wrote words with her web.

_____

6. A girl played the part of Charlotte her costume was black.

_____

_____

7. Looked like a giant spider.

_____

Capital Letters for Proper Nouns

> Remember that a proper noun names a particular place, holiday,
> day of the week, or month.
> Capitalize the first letter of each important word in a proper noun.
> *Examples:*
>
> United States   Fourth of July   Wednesday

DIRECTIONS > **Write each sentence correctly. Add capital letters where they are needed.**

1. Americans celebrate independence day on july 4.

_____

2. People in canada celebrate their country's birthday in july, too.

_____

3. It's called dominion day or canada day.

_____

4. On july 1, 1867, canada gained its independence.

_____

5. Two special holidays are celebrated in mexico.

_____

6. Both september 16 and may 5 call for parades and speeches.

_____

7. Next monday, september 3, we will celebrate labor day.

_____

8. Flags will be displayed on cherry street.

_____

Capital Letters for Names and Titles of People and Pets

> Begin each part of the name of a person with a capital letter.
> Begin a title of a person, such as *Ms., Mrs., Mr.,* or *Dr.,* with a capital letter.
> Always capitalize the word *I.*
> *Examples:*
> Tony Treworgy
> Dr. Vera Wesley
> I know I have a dentist appointment today.

DIRECTIONS ▶ **Write each sentence correctly. Add capital letters where they are needed.**

1. sherman smith has an unusual nickname.

_____

2. Someone took cindi's doll.

_____

3. the only suspect is mr. treworgy.

_____

4. mrs. sample does not have the doll.

_____

5. dr. carter treated a boy the same morning.

_____

6. sherman asked capt. kent for help.

_____

7. Did you see where i left my doll?

_____

8. i cannot believe that i lost it.

_____

Using Capital Letters

Use a capital letter to begin the first word of a sentence.
Use a capital letter to begin the first word, the last word, and all other important words in the title of a book, a story, a magazine article, a poem, a song, or a television show.
Examples:

> Today we solved some arithmetic problems.
> <u>Millions of Cats</u> (book)
> "Numbers and You" (story)

DIRECTIONS → **Read each sentence. Circle the letters that should be capital letters.**

1. school started last week.

2. this year I have a new teacher.

3. her name is Ms. Aarvig.

4. she has given us some interesting arithmetic problems.

5. the problems took a long time to solve.

6. the answers we got were really amazing.

7. One of my favorite books is <u>the amazing number machine</u>.

8. My brother is reading the story "the math magician."

9. My teacher read aloud the article "it all adds up."

10. Have you ever read the poem "crazy eights"?

11. Another good book is <u>math curse</u>.

12. The author also wrote <u>the true story of three little pigs</u>.

Periods

Use a **period (.)** at the end of a declarative or imperative sentence.
Use a period after an abbreviation.
Use a period after an initial.
Use a period after the numeral in a main topic and after the capital letter in a subtopic of an outline.

Examples:
> Arithmetic adds up to answers.
> U.S.   Tues.   Oct.   Dr.   Mrs.
> Jason M. Dawson
> I. How to Master Multiplication
>   A. Learn multiplication tables
>   B. Practice doing multiplication problems

DIRECTIONS   Correct each item. Add periods where they are needed.

1. The new arithmetic books are red and yellow

2. Arithmetic is my first class every morning

3. I have to wake up early to get to class on time

4. Pages full of arithmetic problems are a challenge

5. Mrs Washington is my arithmetic teacher this year

6. Sometimes Dr Carver attends our class

7. Ryan B Right is the smartest boy in my arithmetic class

8. T C Russell won an award at the arithmetic fair

9. I shared my book today with J D Kline

10. I   Arithmetic Every Day
    A   In the classroom
    B   At home
    C   At the store

Abbreviations and Initials

An **abbreviation** is a short way of writing a word or words.
Use capital letters and periods to write most abbreviations.
An **initial** is an abbreviation of a name. The initial is the first letter
of the name.
Use capital letters and periods to write an initial.
Examples:

Doctor = *Dr.*	Avenue = *Ave.*
Tuesday = *Tues.*	January = *Jan.*
Tina Latisha Evers = *T. L. Evers*	

DIRECTIONS Rewrite the following items. Use abbreviations and initials whenever possible.

1. Doctor Jennifer Frances Newsome _____

2. 1623 Plateau Drive _____

3. Thursday, November 10 _____

4. Senator Margaret Jackson _____

5. Captain Marcos Manuel Uribe _____

6. Saturday, September 30 _____

7. 403 Jungle Boulevard _____

8. Tuesday, August 18 _____

DIRECTIONS Write each item correctly.

9. mrs r v Toliver _____

10. 2204 Mountain ave _____

11. wed, apr 27 _____

12. mr a c Hwang _____

Using Commas

Use a **comma (,)** after the words *yes* and *no* when they begin a statement.
Use a comma after time-order words such as *first, next, then,* and *last.*
Use commas to separate three or more words in a series.
Use a comma before the word *and, but,* or *or* when two sentences are combined.
Use a comma to separate a word used in direct address from a sentence.
Use a comma between a quotation and the rest of the sentence.
Examples:
>   *Yes,* the boys should join their father.
>   *First,* the boys must have a plan.
>   The boys ran *quickly, silently, and anxiously.*
>   Josh felt tired, *but* he continued to run.
>   *"Andy,* I need to rest for a minute."
>   *"We are almost there,"* said Andy.

DIRECTIONS ▶ **Read each sentence. Add commas where they are needed.**

1. Yes Mr. and Mrs. Saxby helped the boys.

2. First he told them about the plan.

3. The boys studied letters words and maps.

4. Mr. Saxby talked about Searsville Richmond Washington and Philadelphia.

5. Mr. Saxby had a map but the boys lost it.

6. Mrs. Saxby pasted a label on a jar and she put jelly in it.

7. "Andy you must pretend that this is not yours."

8. "Travel by day" said Mr. Saxby.

Commas in a Series

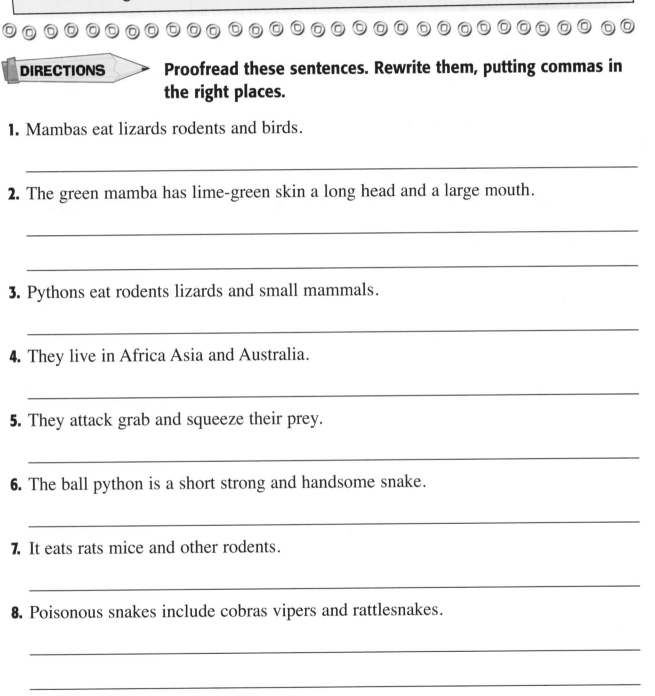

Use a **comma (,)** after each item except the last one in a series of three or more items.
Example:
The green mamba snake is *beautiful, swift, and deadly.*

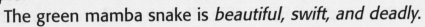

DIRECTIONS ▶ **Proofread these sentences. Rewrite them, putting commas in the right places.**

1. Mambas eat lizards rodents and birds.

_____

2. The green mamba has lime-green skin a long head and a large mouth.

_____

3. Pythons eat rodents lizards and small mammals.

_____

4. They live in Africa Asia and Australia.

_____

5. They attack grab and squeeze their prey.

_____

6. The ball python is a short strong and handsome snake.

_____

7. It eats rats mice and other rodents.

_____

8. Poisonous snakes include cobras vipers and rattlesnakes.

_____

_____

More Uses for Commas

Use a **comma (,)** in an address to separate the city and state or the city and country.
Use a comma between the day and the year.
Use a comma after the greeting of a friendly letter and after the closing of any letter.
Examples:

Anchorage, Alaska   Paris, France
March 19, 2005   Monday, January 27, 2005
Dear Gramma,
Your granddaughter,

DIRECTIONS **Write each item correctly. Add commas where they are needed.**

1. Lone Star Texas 75668 _____

2. November 15 2005 _____

3. Winter Park Florida 32792 _____

4. August 2 2005 _____

5. Juneau Alaska 99673 _____

6. December 23 2005 _____

7. Dear Aunt Rita _____

8. Sincerely yours _____

9. Dear Mother _____

10. Your friend _____

11. Dear Mika _____

Question Marks and Exclamation Points

Use a **question mark (?)** at the end of an interrogative sentence.
Use an **exclamation point (!)** at the end of an exclamatory sentence.
Examples:
> Who stole the roller skates?
> I cannot imagine stealing from a detective!

 **DIRECTIONS** ▷ **Finish each sentence with the correct end punctuation mark.**

1. Do you enjoy reading mysteries

2. They are also exciting to read

3. Which mystery writers are your favorites

4. Donald Sobol writes terrific mysteries

5. Have you ever read the mystery series about Amy Adams and Hawkeye Collins

6. Nancy Drew mysteries are the greatest

7. How does Nancy solve her mysteries so quickly

8. She is a natural sleuth

9. Would you like to be a detective

10. What case would you like to solve first

11. What a great way to start

12. What is the case

13. How about helping me find my keys

14. What a funny detective you are

Colons and Apostrophes

Use a **colon (:)** between the hour and the minute in the time of day.
Use an **apostrophe (')** to show that one or more letters have been left out in a contraction.
Add an apostrophe and an *s* to singular nouns to show possession.
Add an apostrophe to plural nouns that end in *s* to show possession.
Add an apostrophe and *s* to plural nouns that do not end in *s* to show possession.
Examples:

2:35 PM	7:10 AM
was not = *wasn't*	did not = *didn't*
Erika's parka	the *cat's* whiskers
guests' laughter	*boys'* plan
women's advice	*children's* schoolwork

DIRECTIONS ▷ **Correct each sentence. Add apostrophes and colons where they are needed.**

1. Erika s birthday was on a cold winter day.

2. The children s faces lit up when they saw the snow.

3. The two girls walk home was difficult.

4. Her mother s voice greeted Erika.

5. "We don t have everything for your party."

6. "I ll go with you to the store," Erika replied.

7. "Where s Father?" Erika asked.

8. "We ll look for your father on the way to the store."

9. She added, "Father left at 6 30 this morning."

10. "I left school at 3 15 this afternoon," said Erika.

Contractions with *Not*

A **contraction** is a short way of writing two words together. Some of the
letters are left out. An apostrophe takes the place of the missing letters.
Use verbs and the word *not* to form some contractions.
Examples:

could + not = *couldn't*   had + not = *hadn't*   will + not = *won't*

DIRECTIONS  Replace the words in ( ) with a contraction. Write the
contraction on the line.

1. Libby _____ ever visited Log Cabin Village before.
(had not)

2. She _____ believe how small the cabins were.
(could not)

3. It _____ easy to imagine how a whole family could have
(was not)
lived in one.

4. "I _____ understand how they kept warm in the winter," she said.
(do not)

5. "You just _____ noticed the fireplace," Brad answered.
(have not)

6. It _____ have been easy to cook over an open fire.
(must not)

7. "The lives of pioneers _____ easy," Libby remarked.
(were not)

8. "You _____ imagine that they bought all their clothes at stores,"
(should not)
Brad told her.

9. "I just _____ go until I watch the lady in the pioneer costume
(cannot)
work her spinning wheel," Libby said.

10. "She _____ stop until she has spun all that wool into yarn."
(will not)

Direct Quotations and Dialogue

Use a **direct quotation** to tell a speaker's exact words.
Use **quotation marks (" ")** before and after the words a speaker says.
Begin the first word a speaker says with a capital letter. Put
end punctuation before the ending quotation marks. Begin
a new paragraph each time the speaker changes.
Examples:
> Mom asked, "Where have you been?"
> "I went to the library," Ed said.

DIRECTIONS ➤ **Rewrite each sentence. Add quotation marks and other punctuation where needed.**

1. How would you like to paddle a canoe through a swamp asked Mr Vasquez

_____

_____

2. Tyler asked Will we see any alligators

_____

3. Mr Vasquez answered We might see some deer and bobcats

_____

_____

4. Why does swamp water look brown asked Carla

_____

5. It gets its color from plants in the water Megan explained

_____

_____

6. Ray asked What kinds of plants grow in swamps

_____

7. One unusual plant is the neverwet Mr Vasquez said

_____

Titles

Underline the title of a book or a television show.
Use quotation marks before and after the title of a story, a poem, or a song.
Begin the first word, last word, and all other important words in a title with
a capital letter.

Examples:

<u>My New Kitten</u> (book)
<u>It's a Dog's Life</u> (television show)
"Wind in the Treetops" (story)
"Noses" (poem)

 **DIRECTIONS** **Complete the sentences correctly. Add quotation marks where they are needed.**

1. Dad is bringing home a puppy today, Trudi said.

2. What kind of puppy will he choose? asked Chris.

3. Trudi said, I asked for a pug.

4. Where is my puppy? Trudi asked.

5. Go into the yard, Trudi, her mother replied.

6. Is it in the yard? Trudi asked eagerly.

7. Trudi wrote a poem called My Puppy.

8. She read a story called Our Dog Digger.

DIRECTIONS **Read the sentences. Add underlines where they are needed.**

9. Trudi read the book How to Be a Good Master.

10. Then, she watched the television show Lassie.

11. She read The Alphabet Book to her baby brother.

12. Next, she will read A Trip to the Zoo to him.

Compound Words

> A **compound word** is formed by putting together two smaller words. The first word in a compound word usually describes the second.
> *Examples:*
>   play + ground = *playground*
>   bed + room = *bedroom*

DIRECTIONS Use two words from the box below to make the compound word that is missing in each sentence. Write the compound word.

work	night	over	road	stairs	spreads	up
men	fire	wall	place	rail	bed	paper

My aunt owns a hotel next to an old **(1)**_____ where trains used to run. Long ago, **(2)**_____ who were building the track stayed at the hotel. Now most of the **(3)**_____ guests are tourists. When visitors go **(4)**_____ to the second floor, they find charming, old-fashioned rooms. My aunt has covered the walls of each room with flowered **(5)**_____. Quilted **(6)**_____ decorate the beds and keep guests warm on cool nights. Visitors sit in front of a cozy **(7)**_____ on winter nights and toast marshmallows.

DIRECTIONS Write a sentence with each compound word.

8. watermelon _____

9. roadside _____

10. workshop _____

Synonyms

A **synonym** is a word that has almost the same meaning as another word. When a word has several synonyms, use the one that works best in the sentence.

Examples:

    Jobs is a synonym of *tasks.*   *End* is a synonym of *finish.*

DIRECTIONS ▷ Write a synonym for the underlined word in each sentence.

1. Pioneers had to be very <u>brave</u>.

Synonym: _____

2. Pioneers faced many <u>hardships</u>.

Synonym: _____

3. Thanks to their help, many new cities <u>grew</u>.

Synonym: _____

4. The mountain men played an <u>essential</u> role.

Synonym: _____

5. Mountain men <u>relied</u> on their horses and guns.

Synonym: _____

6. Native Americans often <u>assisted</u> the mountain men.

Synonym: _____

7. <u>Stories</u> of the pioneers live on today.

Synonym: _____

8. They succeeded in finding great <u>opportunities</u>.

Synonym: _____

9. We still read stories of their <u>journeys</u> west.

Synonym: _____

10. You will probably learn about them in your history <u>course</u>.

Synonym: _____

Antonyms

An **antonym** is a word that means the opposite of another word.
When a word has more than one antonym, use the one that expresses your meaning exactly.

Examples:

Hard is an antonym of *soft.*   *Short* is an antonym of *tall.*

DIRECTIONS > **Complete each sentence by writing an antonym of the word in ( ).**

1. Josh has been reading a very _____ book about inventions.
   (boring)

2. He learned that sometimes an invention that seems _____ turns
   (great)
   out to be important.

3. Early zippers didn't stay _____ very well.
   (open)

4. Some jigsaw puzzles were developed to make learning geography
   more like _____.
   (work)

5. Earmuffs were invented by a teenager whose ears felt _____
   (comfortable)
   in cold weather.

DIRECTIONS > **Complete each sentence, using an antonym for the underlined word.**

6. Josh would like to invent a <u>cheap</u> model airplane, but _____

   _____

7. He hoped the work would go <u>quickly</u>, but _____

   _____

8. Drawing the plans is <u>complicated</u>, but _____

   _____

Prefixes

A **prefix** is a letter or group of letters added to the beginning of a base word. A base word is a word to which other word parts may be added. Adding a prefix to a word changes the word's meaning.
Examples:
> The prince said he *liked* being in the cave.
> He *disliked* the way the kingdom was run.

Prefix	Meaning	Example
dis	not	dislike
im	not	impossible
in	not	inactive
mis	incorrectly	mislabel
non	not	nonstop
pre	before	prepay
re	again	reread
re	back	repay
un	not	unkind
un	opposite of	unbutton

DIRECTIONS Read each sentence. Add a prefix with the meaning in ( ) to each underlined word. Write the new word on the line. Use the list above to help you.

1. Tony was <u>fair</u> to keep the doll. _____
(not)

2. He waited <u>patiently</u> for Cindi's reaction. _____
(not)

3. Sherlock <u>planned</u> how he would look for the doll. _____
(before)

4. Tony <u>understood</u> Sherlock's interest in the doll. _____
(incorrectly)

5. Tony <u>covered</u> the doll's hiding place. _____
(opposite of)

6. Sherlock <u>traced</u> Tony's path. _____
(again)

7. She thought he was <u>capable</u> of finding the doll. _____
(not)

Suffixes

A **suffix** is a letter or group of letters added to the ending of a base word. A base word is a word to which other word parts may be added. A suffix changes the meaning of a word.

Examples:

The tired hik<u>er</u> rested quiet<u>ly</u>.

Suffix	Meaning	Example
al	like, referring to	coast<u>al</u>
able, ible	able to be	break<u>able</u>, flex<u>ible</u>
er, or	one who	sing<u>er</u>, sail<u>or</u>
ful	full of	help<u>ful</u>
less	without	home<u>less</u>
y	what kind	snow<u>y</u>
ly	how	quick<u>ly</u>
ist	one who does	art<u>ist</u>

DIRECTIONS Add a suffix from the box to the word in ( ). Write the new word to complete the sentence.

able	er	ful	less	or	y

1. I attended a very _____ concert.
(enjoy)

2. The guest _____ seemed to have a good time.
(conduct)

3. As he conducted, his movements were _____.
(grace)

4. A popular _____ joined the orchestra for one song.
(sing)

5. Another number featured a solo by a famous guitar _____.
(play)

6. The medley of tunes by George Gershwin was peaceful and _____.
(dream)

Homographs

Homographs are words that have the same spelling but different meanings.
Some homographs are pronounced differently.
Examples:
Some animals *live* on land and water.
Live plants are not allowed in this building.

DIRECTIONS ➤ Write the homograph from the box that completes each sentence. On the line before the sentence, write the number of the definition for the homograph in that sentence.

---

bass¹—a kind of fish   bass²—a low-pitched sound
slip¹—a small piece   slip²—to slide accidentally
roll¹—a small piece of bread   roll²—to move by turning over and over
wind¹—moving air   wind²—to turn around and around

_____ **1.** Be careful not to _____ on the icy sidewalk.

_____ **2.** The _____ made the kite fly high.

_____ **3.** My baby sister has learned to _____ a ball.

_____ **4.** He wrote his name on a _____ of paper.

_____ **5.** I caught a large _____ at Greenway Lake.

_____ **6.** The paths _____ around the mountain.

_____ **7.** Do you put butter on your _____?

_____ **8.** My brother sings _____ in the choir.

DIRECTIONS ➤ Write a sentence that shows one meaning of this homograph: *rock.*

_____

_____

Homophones

Homophones are words that sound alike but are spelled differently and have different meanings.

Example:

Beth did the *right* thing to help her allergy.
Did she *write* a thank-you note to the doctor?

"Please *be* my friend!" Beth begged.
Beth was not allergic to *bee* stings.

 **DIRECTIONS**   Complete each sentence correctly. Choose the correct homophone in ( ) and write it in the blank.

1. The dirt road leading to the farm _____ the highway.
(meats, meets)

2. The girl _____ the sign that told her about the puppies.
(red, read)

3. _____ the man sell her a puppy?
(Would, Wood)

4. The girl thought it would be hard to _____ a puppy.
(choose, chews)

5. The girl thought she could _____ her mother.
(hear, here)

6. When she reached the turn, she saw her _____ yellow house.
(pail, pale)

7. Her mother said she _____ nothing about any puppies.
(new, knew)

8. The puppy wagged its _____.
(tail, tale)

9. It would _____ for the girl to come home from school.
(wait, weight)

10. The puppy jumped on her when it _____ its name.
(herd, heard)

Homophones

Troublesome Words

Use **too** when you mean "more than enough" or "also." Use **to** when you mean "in the direction of." Use **two** when you mean the number.
Examples:

Washington State is *too* beautiful for words!

I've never been *to* the Northwest.

My aunt and uncle went there for *two* weeks.

Use **it's** when you mean "it is." Use **its** when you mean "belonging to it."
Examples:

It's a good day to carve a totem pole.

A totem pole has many figures on *its* body.

DIRECTIONS Complete each sentence correctly by writing *to, too,* or *two.*

1. Long ago, the Kwakiutl people came

_____ the Northwest.

2. No _____ of their beautiful masks

look alike.

3. The masks were never worn _____

daily events.

4. The masks seem _____ heavy to me.

DIRECTIONS Complete each sentence correctly by writing *it's* or *its.*

5. When I see the log, _____ size surprises me.

6. _____ huge and heavy.

7. Small knots cover _____ surface.

8. I try to carve a bird, but _____ not very good.

Troublesome Words, page 2

Use **your** when you mean "belonging to you." Use **you're** when you mean "you are."
Examples:
> *You're* welcome to join our quilting group.
> Don't forget to bring *your* sketches next week.

Use **their** when you mean "belonging to them." Use **there** when you mean "in that place." Use **they're** when you mean "they are."
Examples:
> *Their* "brains" are really computers.
> I like that little robot over *there*.
> *They're* small, silver, and smart.

DIRECTIONS Complete each sentence correctly by writing *your* or *you're*.

1. I hear that _____ a good nature artist.

2. Is _____ brother talented, too?

3. Did _____ family teach you how to do this?

4. Allen says _____ making a quilt.

DIRECTIONS Circle the correct word in ( ) to complete each sentence.

5. Robots are loyal to (they're / their) owners.

6. (Their / They're) good to have nearby.

7. That one over (there / their) has been in the family for years.

8. (Their / They're) the perfect helpers.

9. Robots are worth (their / they're) weight in metal.

Negatives

A **negative** is a word that means "no" or "not."
The words *never, no, nobody, none, not, nothing,* and *nowhere* are negatives.
The negative word *not* is often used in contractions.
Do not use two negatives in the same sentence.
Examples:
> Joe had *never* worked in a factory before.
> *Nobody* there knew him.
> He *didn't* know at first how hard the work was.

DIRECTIONS ➤ Write the word in ( ) that makes the sentence correct.

1. George Washington didn't _____ live in the White House.
(ever, never)

2. The government didn't have _____ special place for the
(any, no)
president to live.

3. There _____ no official home for the president until 1800.
(was, wasn't)

4. The White House wasn't ready for _____ to live in until John
(nobody, anybody)
Adams was president.

5. Even then, the house didn't have _____ rooms that were
(any, no)
completely finished.

6. President Jefferson didn't waste _____ time before improving
(any, no)
the White House.

7. There _____ no terraces at the ends of the building until his time.
(were, weren't)

8. Only a few presidents didn't do _____ to change the White House.
(anything, nothing)

9. There haven't been _____ who were completely satisfied with
(any, none)
the house.

10. The White House doesn't belong to _____ certain president.
(any, no)

Avoiding Wordy Language

Good writers say what they mean in as few words as possible. When you revise, cross out words that don't add to the meaning.
Example:

Mo made an attempt to jump out of the boat he was in.   (wordy)
Mo tried to jump out of the boat.   (better)

DIRECTIONS   **Rewrite the story. Take out the underlined words or replace them with fewer words that mean the same thing.**

Dove was <u>putting on her clothes and getting ready</u> for Wren's party. How <u>puffed up and proud</u> she was of her snowy white dress! It <u>might possibly</u> be the most beautiful outfit <u>of all the birds that had been invited to the party</u>. Dove turned around and around. She admired <u>the reflection of herself</u> in the mirror. "How lovely I look!" she cried. <u>Just about at that time</u> her wing bumped <u>up against</u> a bottle of ink that was sitting on her desk. The <u>little bottle of ink</u> turned over, and splash! Down the front of <u>the white dress that Dove was wearing</u> went an inky black stain.

Moral: Be proud of yourself, but <u>be careful not to be</u> more proud than you should be.

_____

_____

_____

_____

_____

_____

_____

_____

_____

_____

Avoiding Wordy Language

Adding Describing Words to Sentences

Good writers choose describing words to create clear, strong pictures.
Examples:
> The new coin was *shiny* and *bright.*
> The dog's fur was *soft* and *smooth.*

DIRECTIONS Replace each word in ( ) with a vivid and exact describing word. Use words from the box, or use other words.

lovely	silent	fabulous	precious
ear-splitting	frantic	peaceful	colorful
towering	bustling	gentle	glistening

1. The valley was a _____ place.
(quiet)

2. Nestled in the _____ Rockies, it was blanketed with
(high)
_____ snow much of the year.
(shiny)

3. In the summer, green grass and _____ flowers covered the hillsides.
(pretty)

4. Deer grazed there as _____ breezes whispered.
(slow)

5. Then one day, _____ gold was discovered in the
(valuable)
_____ valley.
(nice)

6. Thousands of people rushed to find _____ riches.
(great)

7. Suddenly, Caribou turned into a _____ city.
(busy)

8. The valley was filled with the _____ noise of
(loud)
_____ miners searching for gold.
(eager)

Using Metaphors and Similes

Writers can create vivid word pictures by comparing two things that are not usually thought of as being alike. When *like* or *as* is used to compare two things, the comparison is called a **simile**. A **metaphor** makes a comparison by speaking of one thing as if it were another. *Examples:*

His feet smelled <u>like</u> dead fish.
Paul Bunyan was as big <u>as</u> a tree.
The *hot room* was an *oven*.

DIRECTIONS ➤ Read the paragraph. Then, complete the sentences.

The deep lake was a golden mirror reflecting the setting sun. As a large ball of orange wax slowly melting, the sun slipped below the treetops. Across the water, a row of mountain peaks raised jagged teeth to the sky. Beyond the mountains, the sunset blazed like a pink and orange flame.

1. One metaphor compares the lake to _____.

2. Another metaphor compares mountain peaks to _____.

3. One simile compares the setting sun to _____.

4. Another simile compares the sunset to _____.

DIRECTIONS ➤ Complete each metaphor and simile.

5. (metaphor) The white clouds were _____

_____

6. (simile) The warm breeze was like _____

_____

7. (metaphor) The rows of corn were _____

_____

8. (simile) The falling autumn leaves were like

_____

Using Personification

Sometimes a writer will give human characteristics to nonhuman things. Objects, ideas, places, or animals may be given human qualities. They may perform human actions. This kind of language is called **personification**. Personification helps a writer to create an exciting picture in the reader's mind.

Examples:

The clothes on the line danced in the wind.
The flames ate hungrily at the wood.

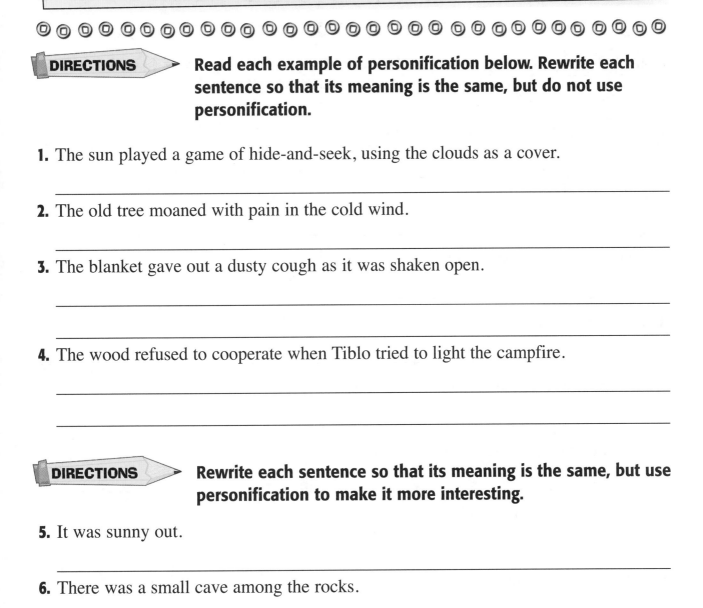

DIRECTIONS ▷ **Read each example of personification below. Rewrite each sentence so that its meaning is the same, but do not use personification.**

1. The sun played a game of hide-and-seek, using the clouds as a cover.

_____

2. The old tree moaned with pain in the cold wind.

_____

3. The blanket gave out a dusty cough as it was shaken open.

_____

_____

4. The wood refused to cooperate when Tiblo tried to light the campfire.

_____

_____

DIRECTIONS ▷ **Rewrite each sentence so that its meaning is the same, but use personification to make it more interesting.**

5. It was sunny out.

_____

6. There was a small cave among the rocks.

_____

Using Figurative Language

Writers often use **figurative language** to compare unlike things. Figurative language uses figures of speech such as similes, metaphors, and personification. Figurative language gives a meaning that is not exactly that of the words used. Figurative language tries to create a clearer word picture for the reader.

Examples:

Mother Nature

Father Time

DIRECTIONS Rewrite each statement below. State the same idea, but use a simile, a metaphor, or personification.

1. A heavy rainstorm fell on the mountain.

_____

2. Daffodils blew in the breeze.

_____

3. A bolt of lightning struck the tree.

_____

4. The round, white moon shone brightly overhead.

_____

5. A wolf howled in the forest.

_____

6. A gentle wind blew across the meadow.

_____

7. The building was very tall.

_____

8. Carl ate a big lunch.

_____

Figurative Language

Paragraphs

A **paragraph** is a group of sentences that tells about one main idea. The first line of a paragraph is indented. This means the first word is moved in a little from the left margin.

The **topic sentence** expresses the main idea of the paragraph. It tells what all the other sentences in the paragraph are about. The topic sentence is often the first sentence in a paragraph.

The other sentences in a paragraph are **detail sentences**. Detail sentences add information about the topic sentence. They help the reader understand more about the main idea.

Example:

Greenland has a very cold climate. This island is located in the northwest Atlantic Ocean near the Arctic Ocean. More than 85 percent of Greenland is covered with an ice sheet, or glacier. This far north, the ice does not all melt during the summer. The summer sun causes icebergs to break off the ice sheet and to float down the rivers.

How to Write a Paragraph

1. Write a topic sentence that clearly tells the main idea of your paragraph.
2. Indent the first line.
3. Write detail sentences that tell about the main idea.

DIRECTIONS Write three detail sentences for the following topic sentence.

In the summer you can have lots of fun.

_____

_____

_____

Keeping to the Topic

Good writers keep to the point when they give information. A good writer plans a paragraph so that it gives details about one main idea.
All the sentences in a paragraph must keep to the topic.

DIRECTIONS ▷ **On the line below each paragraph, write the sentence that does not belong in the paragraph.**

Vehicles called submersibles help scientists explore deep parts of the ocean. Scientists need no special suits for riding in a submersible, since the air pressure inside is the same as at the surface. Some submersibles have mechanical hands for picking up objects on the ocean floor. Scuba divers explore the ocean wearing air tanks.

1. _____

It is true that some rocks can move without any help from humans. Skid marks in the sand in Death Valley show that some big rocks have moved. Death Valley is in California. Scientists believe that rain or freezing temperatures make the desert sand slick enough so that strong winds can push the rocks along the ground.

2. _____

DIRECTIONS ▷ **Use the facts below to write a paragraph. Leave out the fact that does not support the main idea.**

The dingo is a wild dog.
It lives in Australia.
Kangaroos and koalas live in Australia.
Dingoes usually howl instead of bark.
Dingoes can make good pets if they are caught as puppies.

_____

_____

_____

_____

_____

Using Examples

Good writers support their main idea with examples.

DIRECTIONS ➤ **Read the paragraph. Then, answer the questions.**

Good study habits contribute to better grades. Students study more effectively in a quiet room than in a noisy one. When my brother stopped leaving his radio on while he studied, his grades improved from C's to B's. If you want to make better grades, turn off that radio!

1. What is the writer's main idea? _____

_____

2. What example supports the writer's main idea? _____

_____

3. How does the example help the writer's argument? _____

_____

DIRECTIONS ➤ **For each statement, write an example that supports it.**

4. Jumping out of a moving swing can be dangerous. _____

_____

5. A person should always swim with a buddy. _____

_____

6. The library is a good place to spend a rainy afternoon. _____

_____

Narrative

A **narrative** is a story. It tells about real or made-up events. A narrative tells about one main idea. A narrative should have a beginning, a middle, and an end.

Most narratives have **dialogue**. A writer uses dialogue to show how characters speak to one another.

Example:

It was Halloween night, and Teresa was having a party.

Suddenly, there was a loud crack of thunder, and the room went black.

"What happened?" Amy screamed.

"I don't know," Teresa said.

The lights came on again but not in the living room. Then, Teresa had an idea. She lit all the Halloween candles. Teresa's bright idea saved the party.

How to Write a Story and Dialogue

1. Write an interesting beginning to present the main character and the setting.
2. Tell about a problem that the main character has to solve in the middle. Tell about what happens in order.
3. Write an ending. Tell how the main character solves the problem or meets the challenge.
4. Write a title for your story.
5. Place quotation marks before and after a speaker's exact words.
6. Use a comma to separate a quotation from the rest of the sentence unless a question mark or exclamation point is needed.
7. Begin a new paragraph each time the speaker changes.
8. Be sure the conversation sounds like real people talking. Use words that tell exactly how the character speaks.

Narrative, page 2

DIRECTIONS ➤ Read the example narrative on page 96. Then, answer the questions.

1. What is the problem in the narrative?

_____

_____

2. How is the problem solved?

_____

_____

3. Which two characters have dialogue?

_____

_____

DIRECTIONS ➤ Think about a story that you would like to tell. Use the graphic organizer to plan your narrative.

WRITING PLAN

Beginning	Middle	End
Characters: Setting:	Problem:	Solution:

Tips for Writing a Narrative:
• Think about an exciting story to tell your reader.
• Create a realistic setting and characters.
• Organize your ideas into a beginning, a middle, and an end.
• Write an interesting introduction that "grabs" your readers.
• Write a believable ending for your story.

DIRECTIONS Think about a story you would like to tell the readers. Use your writing plan as a guide for writing your narrative.

_____

_____

_____

_____

_____

_____

_____

_____

_____

_____

_____

_____

_____

_____

_____

_____

_____

_____

_____

Descriptive Paragraph

In a **descriptive paragraph**, a writer describes a person, place, thing, or event.

A good description lets the reader see, feel, hear, and sometimes taste or smell what is being described.

Example:

> The girl thought her new doll was beautiful. It had a face that had been painted with bright colors. Its eyes looked lifelike. The clothes of the doll were finely stitched. There were beautiful buttons on the jacket, and soft lace was sewn around the hem of the dress. The shoes were as soft as butter to touch.

How to Write a Descriptive Paragraph

1. Write a topic sentence that clearly tells what the paragraph is about.
2. Add detail sentences that give exact information about your topic.
3. Use colorful and lively words to describe the topic. Make an exact picture for the reader with the words you choose.

 **DIRECTIONS** **Add descriptive words to this paragraph to make it clearer and more interesting to read.**

The girl was worried about her doll. Her _____ brother had wanted to play with the doll. The girl had told him that the doll was too _____ to play with. Now the girl was in school, away from her _____ doll. She had tried to put the doll in a _____ place. But her brother was very _____ and _____. The girl felt _____ thinking of what could happen if her brother found the doll!

Descriptive Paragraph, page 2

DIRECTIONS > Read the example description on page 99. Then, answer the questions.

1. What is the writer describing in the paragraph?

_____

2. What are some words the writer uses that appeal to your senses?

_____

_____

3. What are some descriptions the writer uses to help you imagine the topic?

_____

_____

_____

DIRECTIONS > Think about something that you would like to describe. It could be a thing, a person you know, or something that has happened to you. Write it in the circle. Then, write words on the lines that describe your topic. Use the graphic organizer to plan your descriptive paragraph.

WRITING PLAN

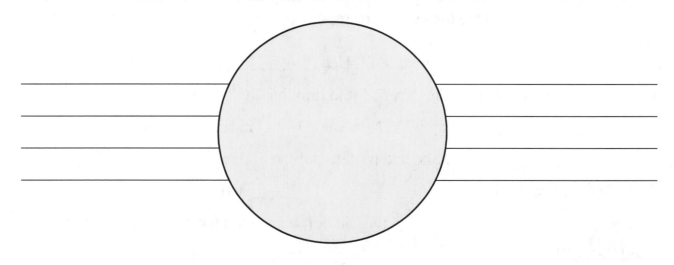

Descriptive Paragraph, page 3

Tips for Writing a Descriptive Paragraph:
- Describe a person, a place, an object, or an event.
- Paint a picture using words.
- Use words that appeal to the reader's senses. Let the reader see, smell, taste, feel, and hear what you are writing about.
- Include a sentence that introduces your topic.
- Write detail sentences that use descriptive words.

DIRECTIONS Think about something that you would like to describe. Introduce your topic in your first sentence. Then, use the words that you wrote in the graphic organizer to describe it. Be sure to appeal to the reader's senses.

_____

_____

_____

_____

_____

_____

_____

_____

_____

_____

_____

_____

_____

_____

Friendly Letter

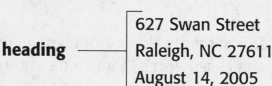

A person writes to someone he or she knows in a **friendly letter**.
A friendly letter has five parts: a heading, a greeting, a body, a closing, and a signature.
Example:

heading — 627 Swan Street
Raleigh, NC 27611
August 14, 2005

greeting — Dear Jason,

body — How is your vacation? I am still selling lemonade. I bought some baseball cards. When you get back, I'll show them to you.

closing — Your friend,

signature — Ben

How to Write a Friendly Letter
1. Write the heading. In the heading, include a comma between the name of the city and the state and between the day of the month and the year.
2. Write the greeting. Capitalize the first letter of each word. End the greeting with a comma.
3. Write a friendly message in the body. Always indent the first line of the body.
4. Write a closing to end the letter. Put a comma after the closing.
5. Sign the letter with your name.

Friendly Letter, page 2

DIRECTIONS Read the example friendly letter on page 102. Then, answer the questions.

1. Who wrote this letter?_____

2. What is the writer's address?

_____

_____

3. What is the greeting of this letter?

_____

4. What is the writer writing about in this letter?

_____

_____

Address an Envelope

An envelope is used to send a letter or a note. The receiver's address goes toward the center. The return address is in the upper left corner. Postal abbreviations are used for state names. The ZIP Code goes after the state abbreviation. *Example:*

Geraldine Roberts
8 Maple Drive
Camp Hill, PA 17011 — **return address**   **stamp**

Joe Canton
15 Talkeetna Road — **receiver's name and address**
Nome, AK 99762

Friendly Letter, page 3

Tips for Writing a Friendly Letter:
- Think of someone to write to.
- Think of something to write about.
- Write your friendly letter.
- Be sure to include all the parts.
- Fill out the envelope correctly.

heading _____

_____

_____

greeting _____

body _____

_____

_____

_____

_____

_____

_____

_____

closing _____

signature _____

How-to Paragraph

A **how-to paragraph** gives directions or explains how to do something. Detail sentences in a how-to paragraph use time-order words to show the correct order of the steps.

Example:

How to Recycle Paper at Home

Help save trees by recycling paper at home. First, gather all your old and unwanted newspapers, magazines, and catalogs. Then, separate the newspapers from the glossy paper inserts. The inserts go with magazines and catalogs to be recycled. Next, place each kind of paper in a separate pile. When you have a bundle that is about 10 inches high, tie it up both lengthwise and around the middle with strong string. Finally, store your paper bundles in a dry place until recycling pickup day. If your community doesn't have a pickup, find out where you can take your paper to be recycled.

How to Write a How-to Paragraph

1. Write a topic sentence that tells what you are going to explain.
2. Add a detail sentence that tells what materials are needed.
3. Write detail sentences that tell the steps in the directions.
4. Use time-order words such as *first, next, then,* and *finally* to show the order of the steps.

How-to Paragraph, page 2

 **DIRECTIONS** Read the example how-to paragraph on page 105. Then, answer the questions.

1. What does this paragraph tell you how to do?

_____

2. What is the first step?

_____

_____

3. What is the final step?

_____

_____

4. What time-order words does the writer use?

_____

 **DIRECTIONS** Think about something you want to tell others how to do. Use this writing plan to help you.

WRITING PLAN

1. What will you tell others how to do?
2. What materials are needed?
3. What steps must the reader follow? Number the steps.
4. What time-order words will you use?

Tips for Writing a How-to Paragraph:
• Choose one thing to teach someone.
• Think of all the materials that are needed.
• Think of all the steps someone should follow.
• Use time-order words to help the reader follow the steps.

DIRECTIONS

Think about something you want to tell others how to do. Use your writing plan as a guide for writing your how-to paragraph.

Information Paragraph

An **information paragraph** gives facts about one topic. It has a topic sentence that tells the main idea. Detail sentences give facts about the main idea.

Example:

Where Does All the Paper Go? — title

When paper is recycled, it doesn't just become recycled paper. It is made into many different new products. — topic sentence

Some of these products include boxes for cereal and shoes. Recycled paper can also be used to make egg cartons, paper towels, and tissues. Some recycled paper helps people send messages to friends and family when it becomes greeting cards. Along with other resources, paper waste becomes plaster boards for the walls of homes and tar paper for under roofs. Even our cars may have paper waste in the form of stiffening for doors and sun visors. — detail sentences

How to Write an Information Paragraph
1. Write a topic sentence that tells your main idea.
2. Write at least three detail sentences that give information about your main idea.
3. Think of a title for your information paragraph.

Information Paragraph, page 2

 **DIRECTIONS** Read the example information paragraph on page 108. Then, answer the questions.

1. What is the main idea of the information paragraph?

_____

_____

2. What are four products made from recycled paper?

_____

_____

3. Write one detail sentence from the paragraph.

_____

_____

_____

 **DIRECTIONS** Think about a topic you would like to write about. Use this writing plan to help you.

WRITING PLAN

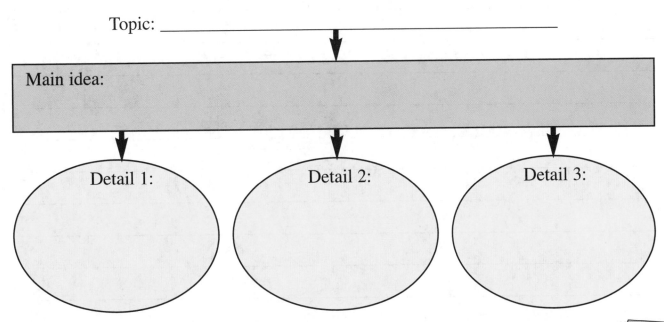

Tips for Writing an Information Paragraph:
• Choose one topic to write about.
• Write a title for your paragraph.
• Write a topic sentence that tells your main idea.
• Write at least two detail sentences that tell facts about the main idea.
• Make sure your facts are correct.

DIRECTIONS → Choose a topic you would like to write about. Use your writing plan as a guide for writing your information paragraph.

_____

_____

_____

_____

_____

_____

_____

_____

_____

_____

_____

_____

_____

_____

_____

_____

_____

Compare and Contrast Paragraph

In a **compare and contrast paragraph**, a writer shows how two people, places, or things are alike or different.

Example:

Colonial Williamsburg and Old Sturbridge Village both show visitors what life was like in the past. Colonial Williamsburg demonstrates life in the 1700s, and Old Sturbridge Village is a recreation of a New England village of about 1830. Both have many shops and other buildings that are open to tourists. Since Williamsburg was an important city in the colony of Virginia, the restored buildings there include the Capitol, the Governor's Palace, and several elegant houses. On the other hand, Old Sturbridge Village gives visitors a taste of life in the country. It includes a farm, a sawmill, and a mill for grinding grain. Popular attractions in both Old Sturbridge Village and Colonial Williamsburg are the demonstrations of crafts that were necessary to life in those times.

How to Write a Compare and Contrast Paragraph

1. Write a topic sentence that names the subjects and tells briefly how they are alike and different.
2. Give examples in the detail sentences that clearly tell how the subjects are alike and different.
3. Write about the likenesses or the differences in the same order you named them in the topic sentence.

Compare and Contrast Paragraph, page 2

DIRECTIONS ➤ Read the example compare and contrast paragraph on page 111. Then, answer the questions.

1. What two things are being compared?

_____

_____

2. How are the two things different?

_____

_____

_____

3. How are the two things alike?

_____

_____

_____

DIRECTIONS ➤ Choose two things you want to write about. Write them on the lines below. Then, use the Venn diagram to help you plan your writing. List what is true only about A in the A circle. List what is true only about B in the B circle. List what is true about both A and B where the circles overlap.

A = _____   A   B   B = _____

Both

Compare and Contrast Paragraph, page 3

Tips for Writing a Compare and Contrast Paragraph:
- Think about your two subjects.
- Decide how the two subjects are alike and different. Choose at least three important similarities and differences.
- Write a topic sentence that tells how the two subjects are alike and different.
- Explain how the two subjects are alike.
- Explain how the two subjects are different.
- Write about the likenesses or the differences in the same order you named them in the topic sentence.

DIRECTIONS ▷ **Choose two subjects you would like to compare and contrast. Use your Venn diagram to write your compare and contrast paragraph.**

_____
_____
_____
_____
_____
_____
_____
_____
_____
_____
_____
_____
_____

Cause and Effect Paragraph

A cause is an event that makes something else happen. An effect is something that happens as a result of a cause. In a **cause and effect paragraph**, a writer first gives a cause. Then, he or she explains what effect or effects happen because of it. One cause may have several effects. One effect may have several causes.

Example:

> The dog was hungry, so it went looking for a bone. The dog knew there were none in the yard, so it began walking up the street. Soon it was far away from home, and it was not sure where it was! The dog had been sniffing the ground, so it did not watch where it was going. It decided to use its nose to find its way back home again. When the dog got there, the boy was so happy to see it that he gave the dog a big bone!

How to Write a Cause and Effect Paragraph
1. Write a topic sentence that tells what happened. Include the cause.
2. Tell the effects of what happened in the detail sentences. Include any new causes, too.
3. Write the detail sentences in the order in which the effects happened.

Cause and Effect Paragraph, page 2

 **DIRECTIONS** → **Read the example cause and effect paragraph on page 114. Then, answer the questions.**

1. What caused the dog to go looking for a bone?

_____

2. What caused the dog to begin walking up the street?

_____

3. What was the effect of the dog's not watching where it was going?

_____

4. What were the two effects of the dog's getting home safely?

_____

_____

 **DIRECTIONS** → **Think of something that happened. What caused it to happen? What were the effects? Use the chart to organize your ideas.**

WRITING PLAN

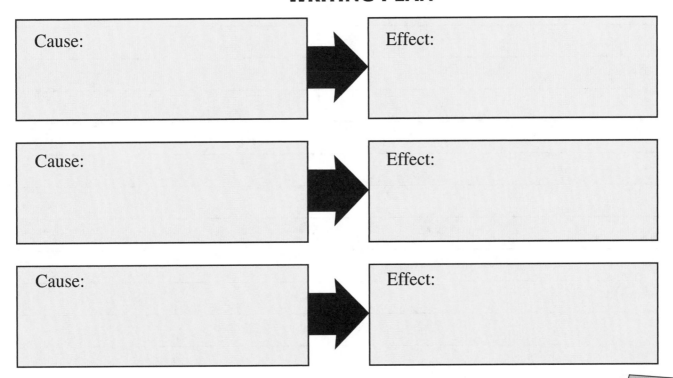

Cause and Effect Paragraph, page 3

Tips for Writing a Cause and Effect Paragraph:
- Think of something that happened. State it in your topic sentence.
- Clearly explain the cause that made something happen.
- Clearly explain the effect that happened because of something else.
- Try to include an end result or effect.

DIRECTIONS Choose an event you would like to write about. Use your writing plan as a guide for writing your cause and effect paragraph.

_____

_____

_____

_____

_____

_____

_____

_____

_____

_____

_____

_____

_____

_____

_____

_____

Book Report

A **book report** tells about the important events in a book. It does not tell the ending. It also gives the writer's opinion of the book. Finally, it says whether others should read the book.

Example:

Go on an Incredible Journey — title of report

The Incredible Journey by Sheila Burnford is — title and author of book
an incredible book. It tells the story of a cat, Tao, — main characters
and two dogs, Bodger and Luath, that set out
across 250 miles of Canadian wilderness — setting
searching for their way home to the family they
love. When the adventure begins, the pets are
staying with a friend while the family is away.
Due to a mix-up, the pets aren't missed for — main events of book
several weeks when they begin their journey. The
pets are chased by wild animals, delayed by
people, and challenged by nature. You'll laugh
and cry as you journey home with these three — whether others should read it
animals. They are courageous and true. This book
is a must for animal lovers.

How to Write a Book Report
1. Tell the title of the book. Underline it.
2. Give the author's name.
3. Tell about the book. Tell the main events. Do not tell the ending.
4. Give your opinion of the book.
5. Think of a title for your report.

Book Report, page 2

DIRECTIONS > Read the example book report on page 117. Then, answer the questions.

1. What is the title of the book? _____

2. Who wrote the book? _____

3. Who are the main characters in the book? _____

4. Where does the book take place? _____

5. Does the writer of the report think others should read the book? _____

DIRECTIONS > Think of a book you would like to tell about. Then, use this writing plan to organize your report.

Title of book: _____

Author of book: _____

Main character of book: _____

Setting of book: _____

Main events of book: _____

_____

_____

_____

_____

_____

_____

_____

_____

Should others read this book? _____

Book Report, page 3

Tips for Writing a Book Report:
- Choose one book to write about.
- Write a title for your report.
- Name the book and the author in your report.
- Name the main character and the setting of the book.
- Tell the main events of the book, but do not tell the ending.
- Tell if you think others would like the book.

DIRECTIONS Choose a book you would like to write about. Use your writing plan as a guide for writing your book report.

_____

_____

_____

_____

_____

_____

_____

_____

_____

_____

_____

_____

_____

_____

_____

Persuasive Paragraph

In a **persuasive paragraph**, a writer tries to make readers agree with his or her opinion.

Example:

> I think students should vote for the lioness as the symbol of our new school. The lioness is intelligent and carries itself with pride. Aren't intelligence and pride in ourselves the qualities we students want to show? Most of all, I think the lioness brings out a feeling of respect in people. People do not usually take advantage of a lioness. By voting for the lioness, we will choose a symbol of intelligence, pride, and respect.

opinion in topic sentence

reasons and facts

strongest reason last

restated opinion or call for action

How to Write a Persuasive Paragraph
1. Write a topic sentence that tells the issue and your opinion about it.
2. Give at least three reasons that will convince your reader to agree with you. Include these reasons in the detail sentences.
3. Explain each reason with one or more examples.
4. Save your strongest reason for last.
5. At the end of your paragraph, tell your feelings again. Ask your reader to feel the same way.

Persuasive Paragraph, page 2

DIRECTIONS > Read the example persuasive paragraph on page 120. Then, answer the questions.

1. What is the writer's main idea in this paragraph?

_____

_____

2. What are two reasons the writer gives to support the main idea?

_____

_____

_____

3. What call for action does the writer have in the last sentence?

_____

_____

DIRECTIONS > Think of something you feel strongly about. Then, use this writing plan to organize your persuasive paragraph.

WRITING PLAN

Main idea: _____

Reason 1: _____

_____

Reason 2: _____

_____

Reason 3 (your strongest reason): _____

_____

Call for action: _____

Persuasive Paragraph, page 3

Tips for Writing a Persuasive Paragraph:
- Choose a topic that you feel strongly about.
- State your opinion in your topic sentence.
- Write good reasons to support your opinion.
- Try to have at least three good reasons.
- Save your strongest reason for last.
- At the end of your paragraph, restate your opinion.
- Tell the reader to take some action.

DIRECTIONS Choose a topic that you have an opinion about. Use your writing plan as a guide for writing your persuasive paragraph.

_____

_____

_____

_____

_____

_____

_____

_____

_____

_____

_____

_____

_____

_____

_____

_____

_____

Writing for a Test

Some kinds of test questions ask you to write. These questions check to see if you can organize your thoughts and express your ideas. They test to see if you can write for a specific purpose and use correct grammar. Here are some tips for writing better on a test.

Before the Test
- Listen carefully to all the directions your teacher or test-giver gives you.
- Read all written directions carefully.
- Ask any questions you have. (You might not be allowed to talk once the test starts.)
- Have several pens or sharpened pencils on hand.
- If you are allowed, read each item on the test before you begin.

During the Test
- Take time to identify your task, audience, and purpose.
- Organize your thoughts before you write.
- Write neatly and clearly.
- Work quietly without disturbing those around you.
- If you need help, raise your hand. Don't call out or get up.

After the Test
- If you finish before time is up, go back and proofread what you have written. Make final corrections.
- Follow directions given at the beginning for what to do at the end of the test. You may have to sit quietly while others finish.

Timed Writing

You have probably taken timed tests before. What are some ways to do well during a timed writing test? Follow these tips to make a timed test go more smoothly:

- Stay calm. Take a deep breath and relax.
- For a writing test, remember to check your task and your purpose. (Unless you are told otherwise, your audience is the person who will read the test.)
- Plan how you will use your time. If this is a writing test, decide how much time you need to spend prewriting, drafting, revising, proofreading, and writing the final draft.
- Use your time wisely once you start writing.
- If you begin to run out of time, decide whether you can combine some steps. Your goal is to finish.

Written Prompts

A written prompt is a statement or a question that asks you to complete a writing task.

- A narrative prompt asks you to tell a story.
- A persuasive prompt asks you to convince the reader.
- An expository prompt asks you to inform or explain.
- A descriptive prompt asks you to describe something.

Picture Prompts

A picture prompt is a statement or question about a picture. It asks you to tell something about the picture. The prompt also tells the purpose for writing.

Using a Dictionary

Each word defined in a dictionary is an **entry word**.

The order of letters from *A* to *Z* is called **alphabetical order**. Entry words in a dictionary are listed in alphabetical order.

There are two **guide words** at the top of every dictionary page. The word on the left is the first entry word on the page. The word on the right is the last entry word. All the other entry words on the page are in alphabetical order between the guide words.

An **entry** is all the information about an entry word.

A **definition** is the meaning of a word. Many words have more than one definition. Each definition is numbered.

A definition is often followed by an **example** that shows how to use the word.

DIRECTIONS   **Use this example dictionary page to answer the questions.**

cherry   **chip**

cher·ry [cher′ē] *n., pl.* **cher·ries**
   1 A small, round, edible fruit, red, yellow, or nearly black in color, and having a single pit. **2** The tree bearing this fruit. **3** The wood of this tree. **4** A bright red color.

child [chīld] *n., pl.* **chil·dren** [chil′dren] **1** A baby. **2** A young boy or girl. **3** A son or daughter. **4** A person from a certain family.

1. What are the two guide words on this page? _____

2. How many definitions are given for *cherry*? _____

3. What is definition 2 for *child*? _____

4. Which of these words would come before *cherry* in the dictionary: *carrot*, *corn*, *cactus*, *clover*? _____

5. Would the word *chop* be on this page? _____

Using a Dictionary, page 2

A **syllable** is a word part that has only one vowel sound. Each entry word in the dictionary is divided into syllables.

A **pronunciation** follows each entry word. It shows how to say the word and it also shows the number of syllables in the word.

The **pronunciation key** lists the symbol for each sound. It also gives a familiar word in which the sound is heard. A pronunciation key usually appears on every other page of the dictionary.

a	add	i	it	o͝o	took	oi	oil
ā	ace	ī	ice	o͞o	pool	ou	pout
â	care	o	odd	u	up	ng	ring
ä	palm	ō	open	û	burn	th	thin
e	end	ô	order	yo͞o	fuse	th	this
ē	equal					zh	vision

ə = { a in *above*   e in *sicken*   i in *possible*
      o in *melon*   u in *circus* }

DIRECTIONS → Read each pronunciation. Circle the word that matches the pronunciation. Tell how many syllables are in the word.

1. pär´ kə   party   parka   _____

2. snō   snow   sun   _____

3. mə · shēn´   matching   machine   _____

4. kâr´ ə · bo͞o   caribou   carbon   _____

5. fä´ thər   feather   father   _____

6. sur · prīz   surplus   surprise   _____

7. līt   light   let   _____

8. (h)wāl   wall   whale   _____

Using a Thesaurus

A **thesaurus** is a book that tells synonyms, words that have nearly the same meaning, and antonyms, words that mean the opposite of a word. Many thesauruses are like dictionaries. The entry words are listed in dark print in alphabetical order. Guide words at the top of the page tell which words can be found on the page. Good writers use a thesaurus to find vivid and exact words.

give	goal

glad *syn* cheerful, happy, jolly, joyful, lighthearted, merry, pleased
ant blue, downcast, glum, sad, unhappy

> **DIRECTIONS** Use a thesaurus. Replace each word in ( ) with a synonym or an antonym. Write the new word on the line.

1. Jared is _____ an excellent football player.
(really)

2. The other players on his team don't think he is _____ just
(different)
because he is deaf.

3. It was _____ for Jared to find a team that would accept
(hard)
a deaf player.

4. Jared never became _____ when a team turned him down.
(angry)

5. Now Coach Taylor is _____ that Jared is playing for the Pioneers.
(happy)

6. Jared is _____ the star of the game.
(often)

7. "Jared is the most _____ runner I have ever seen,"
(exciting)
Coach Taylor says.

Using an Encyclopedia

An **encyclopedia** is a set of books that contains information on many subjects. Each book in a set is called a volume. Subjects are arranged in alphabetical order in each volume. Volumes are also arranged in alphabetical order.

Some encyclopedias have a separate index. The index lists the number of the volume or volumes in which information about a subject can be found.

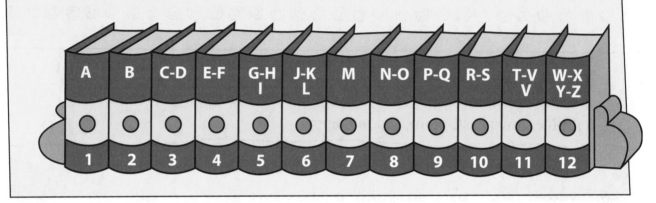

DIRECTIONS Use the example encyclopedia to find the number of the volume in which you would find each of these subjects.

1. Baffin Bay _____

2. Arctic Circle _____

3. penguins _____

4. fur _____

5. North Pole _____

6. kayaks _____

7. Eskimos _____

8. whales _____

9. seals _____

10. ice _____

DIRECTIONS Circle the word or words you would use to find the following information in an encyclopedia.

11. the capital of Greenland

12. animals of the Arctic

13. climate at the South Pole

14. expeditions of Robert E. Peary

15. the average daily temperature in Alaska

ENCYCLOPEDIA

Using the Internet

The computer is a powerful research tool. The **Internet**, a system using telephone and cable lines to send signals, helps you to find almost any information in the blink of an eye. You can communicate instantly with other people by sending electronic mail. Some computers let you see the people as you talk. The key to using the computer as a research tool is knowing what keywords to use to start the Internet search. It takes some practice, but you never know what interesting place you can visit or what information you can find. Here are some hints to speed up the search.

How to Use the Internet
1. Make a list of keywords or names.
2. Choose a search engine that has a directory to narrow the topic.
3. Type in two or three keywords.
4. Type in different combinations of keywords until the topic titles focus on the information you need.

Arts and Entertainment	Games	Reference Materials
Cars and Trucks	Health and Fitness	Science
Computers and Internet	Home and Family	Shopping
	News	Sports

DIRECTIONS ▷ Use the example Internet directory to choose the category you would search for these subjects.

1. astronaut John Glenn _____

2. first aid _____

3. buying a book _____

4. a musical band _____

5. the weather _____

6. how to add fractions _____

7. which Native American groups lived in your area _____

Parts of a Book

The **title page** tells the name of a book. It gives the name of the author. It also tells the name of the company that published the book.

The **table of contents** comes after the title page. It lists the titles of the chapters, units, stories, or poems in the book. It also lists the page on which each new part begins. Everything in the book is listed in the order in which it appears.

An **index** is a list of all the topics in a book. It is in alphabetical order. It lists the page or pages on which each topic appears.

DIRECTIONS Use the example book parts to answer the questions.

A Number of Stories
by
Lisa Newton
 	
Brandywine Arts, Inc.
Chicago, Illinois
	Contents
	
	Adding It Up...............1
	Magic Numbers 10
	Time Tells All 17
	Triple Trouble 42
	Millions of Dimes.....58
		Subtraction
		   fractions 58–60, 119
		   whole numbers, 15, 17–20
		Word problems
		   addition, 2–4, 39
		   division, 40–45, 68
		   multiplication, 25–33, 62
		   subtraction, 35–38, 60

title page	**table of contents**	**index**

1. What is the title of the book? _____

2. Who wrote the book? _____

3. What company published this book? _____

4. What is the first chapter in the book? _____

5. What chapter begins on page 17? _____

6. On what pages would you find facts about fractions? _____

7. What could you learn about on page 39? _____

Reading for Information

Skimming is a quick reading method. When you skim a page in a book, you note its general subject, its divisions, and its major headings.
Scanning is also a quick reading method. When you scan a page, you look for key words.

DIRECTIONS ▷ **Scan the passage to find the answers to the questions below.**

Folk Tales and Fairy Tales

Folk tales and fairy tales are two different kinds of stories. A folk tale tells about the legends and customs of real people. Sometimes America's history is told through the adventures of a folk hero, such as Pecos Bill. However, a fairy tale often takes place in a world of make-believe. "Jack and the Beanstalk," with its giant's castle, is one example of a fairy tale. A character in a fairy tale is often imaginary and sometimes has magical powers. A fairy-tale princess, like Cinderella, has a fairy godmother to grant wishes magically. Even though the two kinds of stories are different, they both always have happy endings.

1. By glancing quickly at the paragraph, how can you tell what it is about?

_____

2. Is "Jack and the Beanstalk" a folk tale or a fairy tale?

_____

3. What is the purpose of a folk tale?

_____

4. Name a fairy-tale princess. _____

5. What are folk characters sometimes based on?

_____

6. Which kind of story has imaginary creatures? _____

7. What kind of ending do folk tales and fairy tales have? _____

Classifying Information

In a research report, good writers limit a topic to one category. They **classify**, or group, details into smaller categories.

DIRECTIONS Imagine that you are going to write a report about animals. Write each of the words below in the possible categories you may use in your report.

polar bear	cow	boa constrictor	dog	jaguar
arctic fox	walrus	bearded seal	sheep	tiger
goat	reindeer	spider monkey	horse	leopard

1. Jungle Animals

_____
_____
_____
_____
_____

2. Animals of the Arctic

_____
_____
_____
_____
_____

3. Domestic Animals

_____
_____
_____
_____
_____

DIRECTIONS Identify the category that was used to group each set of items below. Write the name of the category on the line.

4. _____

sandwich

apple

carrot stick

milk

5. _____

crabs

sharks

sunken ships

coral

6. _____

truck

skateboard

wagon

bicycle

Taking Notes

A writer takes good **notes** to remember the facts he or she finds when doing research for a report.
Example:

<u>Royal Symbols</u> by Crystal Wong, pages 15–16
Who has used the dragon as a symbol?
emperors of China
kings of England

How to Take Notes
1. Write a question. Then, find a book to answer the question.
2. List the title of the book, the author, and the page numbers on which you find information.
3. Write only facts you want to include in your report.
4. Write the information in your own words. Write sentences or short groups of words.

 **DIRECTIONS** The items listed below are from the same pages of the book used for the example notes above. Read each note. Tell whether it answers Question A or Question B.

Question A: What things did the dragon stand for?

Question B: What did the dragon look like?

1. symbol of kindness _____
2. beast with long tail _____
3. symbol of fear _____
4. symbol of power _____
5. similar to a dinosaur _____

Summary

A **summary** is a short sentence or paragraph that tells the main facts or ideas in a story or selection. To summarize any writing, you must pay attention to the details. Using the question words *who, what, where, when,* and *why* can help you find the important details to include in a summary. There are some things you leave out of a summary. That is because they are less important than the main idea and the details. They make the story more interesting, but you can summarize the story or selection without them. A summary table can help you organize the information to write a summary.

DIRECTIONS ▷ **Read the paragraph. Then, complete the summary table.**

People who plan to camp should be prepared for some crawly company. Spiders surprise campers by appearing in unusual places. Spiders might be found on early morning canoe trips. They might jump out of boots, drop from trees, or crawl out from under rocks. Spiders crawl into these different spaces looking for a safe place to spin a web to catch food to eat.

Who:	Summary:
What:	
Where:	
When:	
Why:	

Paraphrasing

Paraphrasing means to restate an idea in your own words. For example, you read a paragraph by another writer. How would you tell the information in the paragraph? You should not copy what the other writer has written. Instead, you would tell the information in your own words. When you do, you paraphrase what the other writer has written.

Example: (you read)

Seals are migrating animals. Fur seals from the Pribilof Islands near Alaska migrate every fall. Female and male fur seals migrate to different places. In the fall, female fur seals swim 3,000 miles to southern California. The male fur seals migrate to the Gulf of Alaska. They travel only 400 to 500 miles from their summer homes.

(you paraphrase): Both male and female fur seals in Alaska migrate, but they go to different places when they do.

 **DIRECTIONS** **Read each paragraph. Then write, in your own words, a sentence or two to tell what the paragraph is about.**

Maureen could hardly believe that she was going to be in fifth grade. She was very excited. But she was nervous, too. The fifth grade was in a different school. The students in her class would be the youngest students in the school. She wondered if the older students would make fun of the younger ones. At the same time, Maureen thought it would be fun to be in a new school. Her stomach was full of butterflies!

1. In your own words, what is this paragraph about?

Maureen discovered that things were not the way she had thought they would be. The new school was large and full of interesting activities. The library was beautiful. The older students were in a different wing. Maureen did not see them often, but when she did, they always smiled at her. Maureen knew that being in the fifth grade was going to be even better than she had imagined.

2. In your own words, what is this paragraph about?

Details

Details are the words and sentences in a paragraph or story that make the selection interesting. They answer the question words *who, what, where, when,* or *why*. Details support the main idea or topic. When taking notes, you should include only details or facts that support the topic of the report or that add interesting information to your writing. A details chart can help you organize the information you read. Then, you can more easily decide which facts should be included in your notes.

DIRECTIONS Read the paragraph. Then, complete the graphic organizer. The first two details have been done for you.

The howler monkeys of South America are very interesting animals. They hardly ever leave the treetops. When they need a drink, they lick damp leaves. The howler monkeys got their name from the noise they make when they are scared. When they sense danger, they make a loud noise that can be heard up to three miles away. Their noise can often scare away what is threatening them.

Topic: How howler monkeys protect themselves	
Question	**Answer**
Who	howler monkey
What	a loud noise
Where	
When	
Why	

Concluding with Details

Sometimes an author may not tell you directly what is happening in a story. You may have to make a **conclusion** based on the facts from the story and on your own experiences or observations. After making a conclusion, though, you may need to change it if additional facts and details are gathered. When taking notes, be sure to note the details. A conclusion must be supported by the details. Using a conclusion flow chart can help you draw the correct conclusion.

How to Draw a Conclusion
1. Read the information carefully.
2. Think about the facts in the resource and your own experiences and observations.
3. Decide what the facts tell you.
4. Change your conclusion if new details show something different.

DIRECTIONS ▷ **Read the paragraph. Then, complete the graphic organizer.**

Tugboats help link the city of Seattle to the sea. The small, strong tugs guide large ships into and out of the harbor. Without the tugs, the big ships could not make the trip safely. To honor the tugs, Seattle holds tugboat races each spring. At that time, the harbor is full of stubby boats splashing in the water like playful whales.

What can you conclude about tugboats?

What details support your conclusion?

1. _____

2. _____

3. _____

Outline

A writer uses an **outline** to organize the information he or she has gathered for a research report.

Example:

> **Royal Dragons**
> I. Symbol of Chinese royalty
>   A. Powerful, kind beast
>   B. Blessed the people
> II. Symbol used by English kings
>   A. Frightening beast
>   B. Represented protection

How to Write an Outline
1. Write a title that tells the subject of your report.
2. Write the main topics. Use a Roman numeral and a period before each topic.
3. Begin each main topic with a capital letter.
4. Write subtopics under each main topic. Use a capital letter followed by a period for each subtopic.

DIRECTIONS ➤ On another piece of paper, organize and write these items in correct outline form.

1. The Falcon
Falcon was symbol of Egyptian King Ramses II
god of the sky
protected the king

2. The Crane
Crane is symbol used in Japan
stands for good luck
used in folk tales

Rough Draft

A writer first puts all of his or her ideas on paper in a **rough draft**.

How to Write a Rough Draft

1. Read your outline and notes. Keep them near you as you write.
2. Follow your outline to write a rough draft. Do not add anything that is not on your outline. Do not leave out anything.
3. Write one paragraph for each Roman numeral in your outline.
4. Write freely. Do not worry about mistakes now.
5. Read over your rough draft. Make notes about changes you want to make.

DIRECTIONS ▷ **Choose one of the outlines below. Write a rough draft of a paragraph for this outline. Include one topic sentence and two detail sentences.**

Bears as Native American Symbols
I. Bear symbolized protection to some Native Americans
   A. Bear masks worn to protect against enemies
   B. Bears in totem poles protected homes

Bears as Symbols of Sports Teams
I. Bear used as symbol in baseball and football
   A. Football—Chicago Bears
   B. Baseball—Chicago Cubs

_____

_____

_____

_____

Research Report

When a writer makes all the changes in the rough draft, he or she writes the final copy of the **research report**.
Example:

Royal Dragons

Many Chinese emperors used a dragon to represent the royal family. The dragon was considered a powerful, kind creature in Chinese myths. People thought the dragon brought them rain, good crops, and good fortune.

Kings of England also chose the dragon for their symbol. They thought the dragon was a frightening beast that would scare the enemy. Long ago, battle shields of the English army had dragons on them. It was believed that a dragon would protect the carriers of the shields.

How to Write a Research Report
1. Write the title of your report.
2. Write the report from your rough draft and your notes.
3. Make all the changes you marked on your rough draft.
4. Indent the first sentence of each paragraph.

DIRECTIONS Read the example research report on this page. Then, choose a topic that interests you, and write your own report. Remember to take notes, make an outline, write a rough draft, and then write your report. Save all your notes to turn in with your report. Your report should be at least two paragraphs long and should have a title.

Topic: _____

Sources: _____

_____

_____

_____

_____

Answer Key

Unit 1

Page 6
Sentences and exact nouns will vary.
1. Tony, family, place, mountains, **2.** Tony, boots, clothes, **3.** fireplace, corner, room, **4.** family, fire, food, **5.** person, ranch, Tony, horse, **6.** path, place, **7.** Tony, dad, things, hike, **8.** animals

Page 7
Common nouns: parents, vacation, car, friends, states, deer, family, week, cousins, trip; Proper nouns: Marcos, Dallas, Texas, Denver, Jackson, Utah, Nevada, California, Bay View Street, San Diego

Page 8
1. kangaroos, **2.** pouches, **3.** types, **4.** animals, **5.** emus, **6.** ostriches, **7.** grasses, **8.** mammals, **9.** otters, **10.** foxes

Page 9
1. animals, **2.** butterflies, **3.** insects, **4.** birds, **5.** skies, **6.** journeys, **7.** rivers, **8.** cities

Page 10
1. children, **2.** men, **3.** pants, **4.** feet, **5.** mice, **6.** geese, **7.** sheep, **8.** deer, **9.** moose, **10.** teeth

Page 11
1. Ms. Kendall's students entered a cooking contest., **2.** All of the class's recipes were original., **3.** Tamisha's pork chops were tasty with applesauce., **4.** Deon's hamburgers were a big hit., **5.** Everyone enjoyed Jennifer's popcorn., **6.** The popcorn's flavor was very spicy., **7.** Mario's pizza won the grand prize., **8.** The pizza's topping was made of fresh vegetables.

Page 12
1. the scarecrows' clothes, **2.** the pumpkins' smiles, **3.** the sisters' hats, **4.** the seeds' flavor, **5.** the plants' stems, **6.** the women's costumes, **7.** the flowers' colors, **8.** the leaves' shapes, **9.** the children's games, **10.** the moose's calves, **11.** the sheep's wool, **12.** the classes' teachers, **13.** the babies' toys, **14.** the drums' sounds

Page 13
1. They; tornadoes, **2.** It; funnel, **3.** them; Scientists, **4.** I; Kayla, **5.** She; Kayla, **6.** He; Grandpa, **7.** him; Grandpa, **8.** You; Phil, Brian

Page 14
1. it, **2.** them, **3.** She, **4.** He, **5.** They, them, **6.** We, **7.** us, **8.** I, you, he, me, **9.** they, I, **10.** They, she

Page 15
He replaces Sequoia, They replaces sequoia trees, It replaces The General Sherman Tree. Sentences will vary.

Page 16
1. Emilia and Miguel visited the zoo with her., **2.** The zoo seemed strange to them., **3.** There were no cages in it., **4.** "I'll show you the giraffes first," their aunt told them., **5.** An ostrich wandered right up to it., **6.** "The ostrich wanted a closer look at us," Emilia laughed., **7.** Monkey Island made a good home for them., **8.** Emilia asked him to take a picture of the monkeys.

Page 17
1. we, **2.** I, **3.** us, **4.** me, **5.** We, **6.** me, **7.** us, **8.** We, **9.** me, **10.** us, **11.** I

Page 18
1. Jason and Jana visited his birthplace., **2.** Its location is near Hodgenville, Kentucky., **3.** His birthplace was a small, one-room log cabin., **4.** Their original cabin has been restored., **5.** Only a few of its original logs are left., **6.** Her climb up the steps to the cabin left her out of breath., **7.** "May I use your camera?" Jason asked Jana., **8.** His cabin is now part of a beautiful park.

Page 19
1. I'd, **2.** It's, **3.** I'm, **4.** He's, **5.** We're, **6.** I'll, **7.** He's, **8.** You'll, **9.** We'll, **10.** they've, **11.** They're, **12.** you're

Page 20
Adjectives in paragraph (articles are not listed): seven, leather, Two, strong, each, many, several, extra, first, long, six, each, new; **1.–4.** Adjectives will vary.

Page 21
1.–12. Adjectives will vary.

Page 22
1. small, dark; cages, **2.** unhappy; visitor, **3.** sorry; He, **4.** large, airy; homes, **5.** content; animals, **6.–10.** Adjectives will vary. Nouns or pronouns are listed. **6.** elephant, **7.** ears, **8.** home, **9.** monkeys, **10.** they

Page 23
1. a, a, **2.** the, **3.** the, **4.** a, **5.** an, **6.** the, **7.** an, **8.** the, a, **9.** an, **10.** an, **11.** an, a, **12.** an, the

Page 24
1. oldest, **2.** older, **3.** prettier, **4.** strangest, **5.** higher, **6.** stranger, **7.** largest, **8.** shinier, **9.** smoothest, **10.** deeper

Page 25
1. most, **2.** more, **3.** more, **4.** more, **5.** more, **6.** most, **7.** more, **8.** most, **9.** more, **10.** most

Page 26
1. worst, **2.** worse, **3.** better, **4.** worse, **5.** worst, **6.** better, **7.** best, **8.** better, **9.** best, **10.** worst

Page 27
1. invented, **2.** have, **3.** came, **4.** revolve, **5.** is, **6.** circles, **7.** was, **8.** estimated, **9.** found, **10.** studied, **11.** took, **12.** showed

Page 28
Responses will vary. Be sure each answer is an action verb.

Page 29
1. playing, **2.** made, **3.** throwing, **4.** collected, **5.** sorting, **6.** received, **7.** collected, **8.** saved, **9.** added, **10.** putting, **11.** display, **12.** won

Page 30
1. have; invited, **2.** are; planning, **3.** is; helping, **4.** will; play, **5.** has; made, **6.** will; tug, **7.** will; fall, **8.** had; said, **9.** had; worried, **10.** will; bring

Page 31
Paragraph: am, reading; has, read; are, settling; has, explored; will, have; are, looking; have, discovered.
1.–6. Helping verbs may vary. Possible responses are given. **1.** were, **2.** had, **3.** am, **4.** will, **5.** was, **6.** have. Sentences will vary.

Page 32
1. is or was, **2.** is or was, **3.** is or was, **4.** were, **5.** was, **6.** were, **7.** am, **8.** was, **9.** were, **10.** was, **11.** was, **12.** am or was

Page 33
Action verbs: invented, write, takes, flopped, barked, splashed; Linking verbs: is, was. **1.** are, **2.** am, **3.** Are, **4.** is, **5.** are, **6.** is. Sentences will vary.

Page 34
1. writes, **2.** imagines, **3.** believes, **4.** mix, **5.** draws, **6.** uses, **7.** fishes, **8.** crushes, **9.** reaches, **10.** flies

Page 35
1. lived, **2.** hiked, **3.** carried, **4.** dipped, **5.** observed, **6.** moved, **7.** studied, **8.** provided, **9.** changed, **10.** worried, **11.** supplied

Page 36
1. will steam, **2.** will chop, **3.** will mix, **4.** will put, **5.** will have, **6.** will stretch, **7.** will learn, **8.** will listen, **9.** will see, **10.** will head

Page 37
1. A blanket of cold air will settle on the valley., **2.** Ms. Asato will read the weather data on her computer., **3.** She will record a warning on an answering machine., **4.** Hundreds of fruit and nut growers will call the line., **5.** Frost will damage young plants and buds on trees., **6.** The growers will work late into the night., **7.** They will roll their huge wind machines into the orchards., **8.** These giant fans will move the air., **9.** The movement of the air will raise temperatures a few degrees., **10.** Wet ground also will keep temperatures higher.

Page 38
1. went, **2.** gone, **3.** seen, **4.** began, **5.** thought, **6.** brought, **7.** said, **8.** began, **9.** made, **10.** went

Page 39
Responses will vary. Be sure each answer contains the verb form shown. **1.** blown, **2.** fallen, **3.** flew, **4.** fell, **5.** dug, **6.** grown, **7.** rode, **8.** ridden, **9.** wrote, **10.** written, **11.** given, **12.** spoken

Page 40
1.–5. Responses will vary. Be sure each sentence includes the adverb in parentheses., **6.–9.** Responses will vary. Be sure each answer is an adverb that tells when or where.

Page 41
Responses will vary. Be sure each sentence includes an adverb from the box.

Page 42
1. more slowly, **2.** most carefully, **3.** steadily, **4.** faster, **5.** more eagerly, **6.** more skillfully, **7.** most skillfully, **8.** more quickly, **9.** most cheerfully, **10.** proudly

Page 43
1. Ben and Me is a humorous book about Benjamin Franklin.; adjective, **2.** The story is amusingly

told from a mouse's point of view.; adverb, **3.** <u>Johnny Tremain</u> is another popular story about early America.; adjective, **4.** It tells about exciting events of the American Revolution.; adjective, **5.** Johnny is a young silversmith.; adjective, **6.** He willingly helps the patriots fight for independence.; adverb

Page 44

1. Lake Slo was a good fishing spot., **2.** correct, **3.** None of the six of us had good luck., **4.** I thought I'd do well because I had my best flies., **5.** correct, **6.** "How did you do that so well?", **7.** correct, **8.** It's not a good idea to be in the hot sun all day without a hat., **9.** correct

Unit 2

Page 45

1. sentence, **2.** Accept completed sentence response., **3.** sentence, **4.** sentence, **5.** Accept completed sentence response., **6.** Accept completed sentence response., **7.** sentence, **8.** Accept completed sentence response.

Page 46

Subjects and predicates will vary. Possible responses: **1.** helps you remember things, **2.** A test, **3.** Social studies, **4.** is the way we communicate, **5.** tells a complete thought

Page 47

1. Sylvie Martin <u>hears the rain on the roof.</u>, **2.** The rain <u>is falling softly.</u>, **3.** The young woman <u>puts on her rain jacket.</u>, **4.** Her shoes <u>are waterproof.</u>, **5.** This person <u>walks toward the beach.</u>, **6.** The streets <u>are quiet today.</u>, **7.** Sylvie <u>steps carefully over puddles.</u>, **8.** She <u>hums softly to herself.</u>, **9.** Her rain jacket <u>keeps her dry.</u>, **10.** Miss Martin <u>is comfortable in the rain.</u>

Page 48

1. fair; The county's fair, **2.** family; My whole family, **3.** games; The games on the midway, **4.** brother; My little brother, **5.** winner; The lucky winner, **6.** tents; Three big tents, **7.** chicken; The finest chicken, **8.** hog; A plump hog

Page 49

1. Sun, sand, **2.** Residents, tourists, **3.** Peace, quiet, **4.** Molokai, Lanai, **5.** forests, canyons, **6.** weather, breezes, **7.–10.** Sentences will vary. Be sure each sentence has a compound subject.

Page 50

Paragraph: Dogs and humans, dogs, humans; Huge hounds and tiny puppies, hounds, puppies; They; Dogs and their owners, Dogs, owners; Dogs; Specially trained dogs, dogs; Guide dogs, dogs; Sled dogs, dogs; Most dogs and their owners, dogs, owners. **1.–2.** Sentences may vary. **1.** German shepherds and Doberman pinschers can be excellent watchdogs., **2.** Children and their parents often enjoy training dogs.

Page 51

Simple predicates will vary. Possible responses are included in the complete predicate. **1.** see some of the most beautiful scenery in America, **2.** reach high into the sky, **3.** stands in central Alaska, **4.** means "the great one.", **5.** is Mount McKinley, **6.** cover much of Alaska, **7.** roam in Alaska's back country, **8.** wanders into town, **9.** is a funny but scary sight, **10.** enjoy fishing in the clear blue lakes and rushing rivers.

Page 52

1. curl, sleep, **2.** stays, cares, **3.** float, sleep, **4.** anchor, float, **5.** sprawls, relaxes; **6.–10.** Responses will vary. Be sure each sentence has a compound predicate.

Page 53

Paragraph: worked hard on the class play, worked; formed committees and made plans, formed, made; discussed the play for hours, discussed; wrote and rewrote the script many times, wrote, rewrote; sounded terrific, sounded; worked hard, too, worked; collected old-fashioned shirts for the cast members, collected; volunteered for the sets committee, volunteered; sketched many different ideas, sketched; chose the best sketch and turned it into a set, chose, turned; hammered, sawed, and painted for many days, hammered, sawed, painted **1.** The actors read the script and memorized their lines. **2.** Everyone in the audience stood up, clapped, and cheered for us.

Page 54

Possible response: Eduardo has always loved the circus, and now he is making plans to become a circus performer. He has taken gymnastics classes, and his teacher is impressed with Eduardo's skill. Eduardo also belongs to a drama club. He likes performing in all kinds of plays, but comedies are his favorite. Soon Eduardo will have to decide which skills to develop. He may become a circus acrobat, or he may decide to become a circus clown.

Page 55

1. Did you know that very few people have been attacked by sharks?; interrogative, **2.** Many types of sharks are not very big.; declarative, **3.** One kind is only about as long as your hand.; declarative, **4.** How can sharks find food in the dark?; interrogative, **5.** They use their senses of hearing, smell, and sight.; declarative, **6.** Some sharks will eat anything.; declarative, **7.** Have you heard that nails, jewels, and even clothing have been found inside sharks' stomachs?; interrogative

Page 56

1. .; imperative, **2.** !; exclamatory, **3.** .; imperative, **4.** .; imperative, **5.** !; exclamatory, **6.** !; exclamatory, **7.** .; imperative, **8.** !; exclamatory, **9.** !; exclamatory, **10.** .; imperative, **11.** .; imperative, **12.** !; exclamatory

Page 57

1. is, **2.** taste, **3.** eat, **4.** were, **5.** was, **6.** tastes, **7.** is, **8.** hold, **9.** takes, **10.** are, **11.** are, **12.** am

Page 58

1. knows, **2.** expect, **3.** find, **4.** surprise, **5.** watches, **6.** moves, **7.** laugh, **8.** speeds, **9.** likes, **10.** show, **11.** admires, **12.** grows

Page 59

Possible response: My parents and I went to Washington, D.C., last year. We left on Monday and drove for three days. I got tired of riding and was glad when we arrived in Washington. Dad took us to the Capitol and showed us our senator's office. Mom loves history and wanted to see the National Museum of American History. I had read about the pandas and asked to go to the National Zoo to see them. We all admire Abraham Lincoln and were thrilled to see the Lincoln Memorial. We had a good time in Washington and learned a lot about our country, too.

Page 60

1. Schools and libraries should have ramps as well as steps., **2.** People in wheelchairs and people on crutches find it hard to climb stairs., **3.** Libraries and other public buildings should have elevators., **4.** Door handles and elevator buttons should be placed low., **5.** People in wheelchairs and everyone else can reach them there.

Page 61

Sentences may vary. Possible responses are given. **1.** Many kinds of spiders spin webs, but not all of the webs are alike., **2.** A web may be long and narrow, or it may be shaped like a triangle., **3.** Some webs are like funnels, but others look more like domes., **4.** Wolf spiders hide in burrows, but lynx spiders live on trees or bushes., **5.** Many lynx spiders are green, and they are hard to find on green leaves., **6.** Tarantulas are furry, and they look fierce.

Page 62

1. Rey-Ling, Karen, and Mitch gave a party., **2.** They met on Monday, Tuesday, and Wednesday to plan the party., **3.** They invited Tina, Mark, and Lee., **4.** Each guest received a paper hat, a balloon, and a new pencil., **5.** The children played Simon Says, Musical Chairs, and Pin the Nose on the Clown., **6.** Mitch, Rey-Ling, and Karen taught the others a new game., **7.** Tina, Lee, and Karen sang a funny song.

Page 63

Answers will vary. Possible responses are given. **1.** wise, **2.** yellow, **3.** grizzly, **4.** bravely, **5.** fierce, **6.** adorable, **7.** cuddly, **8.** white, **9.** sports, **10.** football

Page 64

Possible responses are given. **1.** I went to see a play. It was based on the book <u>Charlotte's Web</u>., **2.** The play had no adult actors., **3.** A boy played the part of Wilbur the pig., **4.** Charlotte was a very smart spider, and Wilbur was her friend., **5.** Charlotte wrote words with her web., **6.** A girl played the part of Charlotte. Her costume was black., **7.** She looked like a giant spider.

Unit 3

Page 65

1. Americans celebrate Independence Day on July 4., **2.** People in Canada celebrate their country's birthday in July, too., **3.** It's called Dominion Day or Canada Day., **4.** On July 1, 1867, Canada gained its independence., **5.** Two special holidays are celebrated in Mexico., **6.** Both September 16 and May 5 call for parades and speeches., **7.** Next Monday, September 3, we will celebrate Labor Day., **8.** Flags will be displayed on Cherry Street.

Page 66

1. Sherman Smith has an unusual nickname., **2.** Someone took Cindi's doll., **3.** The only suspect is Mr. Treworgy., **4.** Mrs. Sample does not have the doll., **5.** Dr.

Carter treated a boy the same morning., **6.** Sherman asked Capt. Kent for help., **7.** Did you see where I left my doll?, **8.** I cannot believe that I lost it.

Page 67
1. School started last week., **2.** This year I have a new teacher., **3.** Her name is Ms. Aarvig., **4.** She has given us some interesting arithmetic problems., **5.** The problems took a long time to solve., **6.** The answers we got were really amazing., **7.** One of my favorite books is The Amazing Number Machine., **8.** My brother is reading the story "The Math Magician.", **9.** My teacher read aloud the article "It All Adds Up.", **10.** Have you ever read the poem "Crazy Eights"?, **11.** Another good book is Math Curse., **12.** The author also wrote The True Story of the Three Little Pigs.

Page 68
1. The new arithmetic books are red and yellow., **2.** Arithmetic is my first class every morning., **3.** I have to wake up early to get to class on time., **4.** Pages full of arithmetic problems are a challenge., **5.** Mrs. Washington is my arithmetic teacher this year., **6.** Sometimes Dr. Carver attends our class., **7.** Ryan B. Right is the smartest boy in my arithmetic class., **8.** T. C. Russell won an award at the arithmetic fair., **9.** I shared my book today with J. D. Kline.,
10.
I. Arithmetic Every Day
 A. In the classroom
 B. At home
 C. At the store

Page 69
1. Dr. J. F. Newsome, **2.** 1623 Plateau Dr., **3.** Thurs., Nov. 10, **4.** Sen. M. Jackson, **5.** Capt. M. M. Uribe, **6.** Sat., Sept. 30, **7.** 403 Jungle Blvd., **8.** Tues., Aug. 18, **9.** Mrs. R. V. Toliver, **10.** 2204 Mountain Ave., **11.** Wed., Apr. 27, **12.** Mr. A. C. Hwang

Page 70
1. Yes, Mrs. and Mrs. Saxby helped the boys., **2.** First, he told them about the plan., **3.** The boys studied letters, words, and maps., **4.** Mrs. Saxby talked about Searsville, Richmond, Washington, and Philadelphia. **5.** Mr. Saxby had a map, but the boys lost it., **6.** Mrs. Saxby pasted a label on a jar, and she put jelly in it., **7.** "Andy, you must pretend that this is not yours.", **8.** "Travel by day," said Mr. Saxby.

Page 71
1. Mambas eat lizards, rodents, and birds., **2.** The green mamba has lime-green skin, a long head, and a large mouth., **3.** Pythons eat rodents, lizards, and small mammals., **4.** They live in Africa, Asia, and Australia., **5.** They attack, grab, and squeeze their prey., **6.** The ball python is a short, strong, and handsome snake., **7.** It eats rats, mice, and other rodents., **8.** Poisonous snakes include cobras, vipers, and rattlesnakes.

Page 72
1. Lone Star, Texas 75668
2. November 15, 2005
3. Winter Park, Florida 32792
4. August 2, 2005
5. Juneau, Alaska 99673
6. December 23, 2005
7. Dear Aunt Rita, **8.** Sincerely yours, **9.** Dear Mother, **10.** Your friend, **11.** Dear Mika,

Page 73
1. ?, **2.** !, **3.** ?, **4.** !, **5.** ?, **6.** !, **7.** ?, **8.** !, **9.** ?, **10.** ?, **11.** !, **12.** ?, **13.** ?, **14.** !

Page 74
1. Erika's birthday was on a cold winter day., **2.** The children's faces lit up when they saw the snow., **3.** The two girls' walk home was difficult., **4.** Her mother's voice greeted Erika., **5.** "We don't have everything for your party.", **6.** "I'll go with you to the store," Erika replied., **7.** "Where's father?" Erika asked., **8.** "We'll look for your father on the way to the store.", **9.** She added, "Father left at 6:30 this morning.", **10.** "I left school at 3:15 this afternoon," said Erika.

Page 75
1. hadn't, **2.** couldn't, **3.** wasn't, **4.** don't, **5.** haven't, **6.** mustn't, **7.** weren't, **8.** shouldn't, **9.** can't, **10.** won't

Page 76
1. "How would you like to paddle a canoe through a swamp?" asked Mr. Vasquez., **2.** Tyler asked, "Will we see any alligators?", **3.** Mr. Vasquez answered, "We might see some deer and bobcats.", **4.** "Why does swamp water look brown?" asked Carla., **5.** "It gets its color from plants in the water," Megan explained., **6.** Ray asked, "What kinds of plants grow in swamps?", **7.** "One unusual plant is the neverwet," Mr. Vasquez said.

Page 77
1. "Dad is bringing home a puppy today," Trudi said., **2.** "What kind of puppy will he choose?" asked Chris., **3.** Trudi said, "I asked for a pug.", **4.** "Where is my puppy?" Trudi asked., **5.** "Go into the yard, Trudi," her mother replied., **6.** "Is it in the yard?" Trudi asked eagerly., **7.** Trudi wrote a poem called "My Puppy.", **8.** She read a story called "Our Dog Digger.", **9.** Trudi read the book How to Be a Good Master., **10.** Then, she watched the television show Lassie., **11.** She read The Alphabet Book to her baby brother., **12.** Next, she will read A Trip to the Zoo to him.

Unit 4

Page 78
Answers may vary. **1.** railroad, **2.** workmen, **3.** overnight, **4.** upstairs, **5.** wallpaper, **6.** bedspreads, **7.** fireplace, **8.–10.** Sentences will vary. Be sure the compound word is correctly written and used.

Page 79
Synonyms may vary.
1. courageous, **2.** difficulties, struggles, **3.** spread, thrived, **4.** key, important, **5.** depended, counted, **6.** helped, aided, **7.** Tales, Legends, **8.** chances, jobs, **9.** travels, trips, **10.** class, book

Page 80
Antonyms may vary.
Possible responses are given.
1. interesting, **2.** small, **3.** closed, **4.** play, **5.** painful, **6.–8.** Responses will vary. Be sure each answer includes an antonym of the underlined word.

Page 81
1. unfair, **2.** impatiently, **3.** preplanned, **4.** misunderstood, **5.** uncovered, **6.** retraced, **7.** incapable

Page 82
1. enjoyable, **2.** conductor, **3.** graceful, **4.** singer, **5.** player, **6.** dreamy

Page 83
1. slip, 2, **2.** wind, 1, **3.** roll, 2, **4.** slip, 1, **5.** bass, 1, **6.** wind, 2, **7.** roll, 1, **8.** bass, 2.
Sentences will vary. Be sure that the homograph is used correctly.

Page 84
1. meets, **2.** read, **3.** Would, **4.** choose, **5.** hear, **6.** pale, **7.** knew, **8.** tail, **9.** wait, **10.** heard

Page 85
1. to, **2.** two, **3.** to, **4.** too, **5.** its, **6.** It's, **7.** its, **8.** it's

Page 86
1. you're, **2.** your, **3.** your, **4.** you're, **5.** their, **6.** They're, **7.** there, **8.** They're, **9.** their

Page 87
1. ever, **2.** any, **3.** was, **4.** anybody, **5.** any, **6.** any, **7.** were, **8.** anything, **9.** any, **10.** any

Page 88
Paragraphs may vary.
  Dove was dressing for Wren's party. How proud she was of her snowy white dress! It might be the most beautiful outfit at the party. Dove turned around and around. She admired her reflection in the mirror. "How lovely I look!" she cried. Then her wing bumped a bottle of ink that was sitting on her desk. The bottle turned over, and splash! Down the front of Dove's dress went an inky black stain. Moral: Be proud of yourself, but not more proud than you should be.

Page 89
Possible responses are given. Be sure responses are appropriate synonyms. **1.** peaceful, **2.** towering, glistening, **3.** colorful, **4.** gentle, **5.** precious, lovely, **6.** fabulous, **7.** bustling, **8.** ear-splitting, frantic

Page 90
1. a golden mirror, **2.** jagged teeth, **3.** a melting ball of wax, **4.** a pink and orange flame, **5.–8.** Responses will vary. Be sure that similes and metaphors are descriptive.

Page 91
Answers will vary. Possible responses are given. **1.** The clouds blocked the sun., **2.** The tree creaked as the wind blew against it., **3.** Dust came out of the blanket when it was shaken., **4.** Tiblo had some trouble getting the fire started., **5.** The sun smiled on Earth., **6.** A small cave was hiding in the rocks.

Page 92
Answers will vary. Possible responses are given. **1.** An army of raindrops attacked the mountaintop., **2.** Daffodils danced gracefully to the music of the wind., **3.** Lightning struck the tree like a flaming spear., **4.** The moon was a bright white balloon floating in the sky., **5.** A wolf sang its sad, lonely song to the forest trees., **6.** A friendly wind skipped across the sleepy meadow., **7.** The building was as tall as a mountain., **8.** Carl ate a ton of food for lunch.

Unit 5

Page 93
Detail sentences will vary.
Be sure that responses pertain to the topic.

Page 94
1. Scuba divers explore the ocean wearing air tanks., **2.** Death Valley is in California.;

The dingo is a special type of dog. It is a wild dog that lives in Australia. Dingoes usually howl instead of bark. They can make good pets if they are caught as puppies.

Page 95
Answers may vary. **1.** Good study habits contribute to better grades., **2.** The writer's brother's grades improved from C's to B's when he studied without the radio., **3.** It shows that quiet studying improves grades., **4.–6.** Responses will vary. Be sure that each answer supports the statement.

Page 97
1. The lights go out at the party., **2.** Teresa lights Halloween candles., **3.** Amy and Teresa

Page 99
Answers will vary.

Page 100
1. a new doll, **2.** bright colors, lifelike eyes, finely stitched clothes, beautiful buttons, soft lace, shoes as soft as butter, **3.** Answers will vary.

Page 103
1. Ben, **2.** 627 Swan Street, Raleigh, NC 27611, **3.** Dear Jason, **4.** summer vacation

Page 106
1. how to recycle paper at home, **2.** gather old and unwanted newspapers, magazines, and catalogs, **3.** store the paper bundles in a dry place until pickup day, **4.** first, then, next, finally

Page 109
1. When paper is recycled, it doesn't just become recycled paper. It is made into many different new products., **2.** Student should name four: cereal boxes, shoe boxes, egg cartons, paper towels, tissues, greeting cards, plaster boards, tar paper, stiffener for car visors and doors, **3.** Answers will vary but should be a detail sentence from the paragraph.

Page 112
1. Colonial Williamsburg and Old Sturbridge Village, **2.** Colonial Williamsburg shows city life in the 1700s, but Old Sturbridge shows country life in the 1830s. The buildings and locations are different, too., **3.** Both show what life was like in the past. Both have many shops and buildings open to tourists. Both have popular demonstrations of crafts.

Page 115
1. It was hungry., **2.** It knew there were no bones in the yard., **3.** It got lost., **4.** The boy was happy, and the dog got a big bone.

Page 118
1. The Incredible Journey, **2.** Sheila Burnford, **3.** Tao, Bodger, and Luath, **4.** in the Canadian wilderness, **5.** yes

]Page 121
1. Students should vote for the lioness as the symbol of our new school., **2.** The lioness is intelligent and carries itself with pride. The lioness brings out a feeling of respect in people., **3.** Vote for the lioness to choose a symbol of intelligence, pride, and respect.

Unit 6

Page 125
1. cherry, chip, **2.** four, **3.** a young boy or girl, **4.** carrot, cactus, **5.** no

Page 126
1. parka, 2, **2.** snow, 1, **3.** machine, 2, **4.** caribou, 3, **5.** father, 2, **6.** surprise, 2, **7.** light, 1, **8.** whale, 1

Page 127
Answers may vary. Be sure answers are appropriate synonyms. **1.** actually, **2.** unusual, **3.** difficult, **4.** upset, **5.** glad, **6.** frequently, **7.** thrilling

Page 128
1. 2, **2.** 1, **3.** 9, **4.** 4, **5.** 8, **6.** 6, **7.** 4, **8.** 12, **9.** 10, **10.** 5, **11.** Greenland, **12.** Arctic, **13.** South Pole, **14.** Peary, **15.** Alaska

Page 129
Answers may vary. **1.** Science, **2.** Health and Fitness, **3.** Shopping, **4.** Arts and Entertainment, **5.** News, **6.** Reference Materials, **7.** Reference Materials

Page 130
1. A Number of Stories, **2.** Lisa Newton, **3.** Brandywine Arts, Inc., **4.** Adding It Up, **5.** Time Tells All, **6.** 58-60 and 119, **7.** addition word problems

Page 131
1. The title tells what the paragraph is about., **2.** fairy tale, **3.** to tell legends and customs of real people, **4.** Cinderella, **5.** real people, **6.** fairy tale, **7.** happy

Page 132
1. jaguar, leopard, boa constrictor, tiger, spider monkey, **2.** polar bear, arctic fox, bearded seal, walrus, reindeer, **3.** dog, horse, cow, sheep, goat, **4.–6.** Answers may vary slightly. **4.** Things in a Lunch Box, **5.** Things in the Ocean, **6.** Vehicles or Things with wheels

Page 133
1. Question A, **2.** Question B, **3.** Question A, **4.** Question A, **5.** Question B

Page 134
Answers may vary. Who: Campers; What: Spiders; Where: In unusual places, such as in canoes and boots; When: At different times; Why: Looking for a safe place to spin a web to catch food; Summary: Spiders spin webs in unusual places to catch food. Campers may be surprised by spiders at any time.

Page 135
Answers will vary. **1.** Maureen had conflicting feelings about going into the fifth grade., **2.** Maureen found that her fears about the fifth grade were needless.

Page 136
Where: in the treetops; When: if they sense danger; Why: to scare away the threat

Page 137
Answers may vary. Possible responses: Conclusion: I can conclude that tugboats are important to the city of Seattle.; Details: **1.** Tugboats guide ships in and out of the harbor., **2.** Tugboats help ships move safely., **3.** The city of Seattle thinks tugboats should be honored because of their importance.

Page 138
The Falcon
I. Falcon was a symbol of Egyptian King Ramses II
   A. God of the sky
   B. Protected the king

The Crane
I. Crane is symbol used in Japan
   A. Stands for good luck
   B. Used in folk tales